Dr. Lutzer's book is a must-read for  the current legal and cultural direction of our nation. Through comparing present-day America with the history of Nazi Germany, Dr. Lutzer paints a chilling picture of what tomorrow could look like in America if we don't take a stand for Christ now.

ALAN SEARS
President, CEO, and General Counsel
Alliance Defense Fund

Woodrow Wilson once spoke of the futility of a nation that forgets its heritage. Erwin Lutzer asks a far more penetrating question: What happens to the nation that forgets God? Using the history of Nazi Germany as his canvas, Lutzer brilliantly illustrates a critically important truth. Just as nature abhors a vacuum, a culture that drives every vestige of God from the marketplace of ideas inevitably finds it has sown seeds that it will reap in the whirlwind.

FRANK WRIGHT, PhD
Former President and CEO
National Religious Broadcasters

ERWIN W. LUTZER

WHEN A NATION FORGETS GOD

7 LESSONS WE MUST LEARN FROM NAZI GERMANY

MOODY PUBLISHERS
CHICAGO

Edited by Elizabeth Cody Newenhuyse
Interior design: Ragont Design
Cover design: The DesignWorks Group
Cover image: Cover photo of hand copyright © Laurent Hamels/GettyImages
    (pha185000004). All rights reserved.

Library of Congress Cataloging-in-Publication Data

Lutzer, Erwin W.
When a nation forgets God : 7 lessons we must learn from Nazi Germany / Erwin W. Lutzer.
    p. cm.
Includes bibliographical references.
ISBN 978-0-8024-1328-4
1. Germany—Church history—1933-1945. 2. Church and state—Germany. 3. Christianity and politics—Germany. 4. National socialism—Religious aspects. 5. National socialism and religion. 6. United States—Forecasting. I. Title.
BR856.L88 2010
274.3'082—dc22

                                                                    2009039288

We hope you enjoy this book from Moody Publishers. Our goal is to provide high-quality, thought-provoking books and products that connect truth to your real needs and challenges. For more information on other books and products written and produced from a biblical perspective, go to www.moodypublishers.com or write to:

Moody Publishers
820 N. LaSalle Boulevard
Chicago, IL 60610

7 9 10 8 6

Printed in the United States of America

CONTENTS

FOREWORD

MY BIOGRAPHY OF Dietrich Bonhoeffer came out in 2010, on the sixty-fifth anniversary of his death. I have ever since been utterly overwhelmed at the response to his story, which it was my privilege to tell. I knew his was an extraordinary life, else I wouldn't have written about it, but the response of readers to that life has been greater than anything I might have hoped. What can account for that response? What do contemporary Americans see in the story of a German pastor that speaks so powerfully to them? For the shortest possible answer to that question, I would simply say, "Read Erwin Lutzer's book!" But since you are already doing just that, let me say a brief word more.

The slightly longer answer is that people have glimpsed in Bonhoeffer's story something disturbingly familiar, something that speaks to us directly, right now. We glimpse ourselves in that story, however dimly, and we are appropriately chilled to do so. In fact, as I have traveled around the United States talking about Bonhoeffer, I have heard people say again and again that what happened in Germany in the run-up to World War II is somehow being repeated in America in our day. I am deeply sorry to agree. Of course the details are different, and to push the parallels too far is to strain credulity and to invite certain and deserved ridicule. We must say that in some ways the differences between that time in Germany and our time in America couldn't be more dramatic. But there are foreboding similarities nonetheless, similarities that demand our fullest attention.

Probably the principal similarity has to do with Religious Freedom. In Bonhoeffer's day, before his very eyes, a robustly Christian nation was swiftly secularized by a powerful government. The church was divided and didn't know what to make of it and they didn't respond as they should have. So the church was overwhelmed by the state, and for all intents and purposes eventually ceased to exist. What resulted from that, among other things, was the Holocaust. What might result from such a thing here in America is unknown, but we should all agree that the slightest movement in that awful direction is cause for alarm. This much we can know: Nothing good can come of it.

We still have tremendous freedoms in this nation, but most Americans are unaware of these freedoms and do not exercise them. This great "experiment in freedom" called the United States of America is not something that is self-sustaining. Freedom is not our natural condition. It is highly fragile and must be defended in every generation. So if we are unaware of what we have, we will not see it slipping away, as it is indeed doing at this time. That is precisely why Dr. Lutzer's excellent book is so important. It clearly and powerfully explains what the parallels are between Germany's fall from grace and the beginning of our own fall. My fondest hope is that it would serve as a loud wake-up call, that we might arrest our terrible fall and begin the journey back to our Foundations. May every American read it and soberly consider everything it says. *Soli Deo Gloria.*

Eric Metaxas
September 2014
New York City

WRITTEN
TO BE READ

IF YOU READ THIS BOOK with the sole intention of finding more grist for your political convictions, then you have missed my heart. Yes, I am deeply distressed over the direction our nation is taking, but I am even more concerned about how the church—the people of God—will react to what is taking place. To become angry, vindictive, and filled with self-pity is hardly what God expects of us. We must respond on many different levels, but surely one of the most important is that we as individuals and the church at large must bear a credible witness to the saving grace of God in Christ.

God is humbling us. The political solutions that we thought would rescue our nation from its moral and spiritual free fall have had scant effect. We are learning that the problem is deeper than we thought, thus the solution itself must be deeper also. In sum, we must realize that only God can save us from those trends that have already evoked His judgment.

As you read these pages, please pay careful attention to the last section of each chapter where I point the reader to scriptural promises and attempt to give encouragement as we face the huge task that confronts us. Although hope fades as we focus only on the trajectory we as a nation have chosen, I pray that hope will rise as we focus on the privilege of living at this time in history when our faith really counts. "May the God of hope fill you with all joy and peace in believing, so that by the power of the Holy Spirit you may abound in hope" (Romans 15:13).

DR. ERWIN W. LUTZER

THE CONTEXT
OF THIS BOOK

YES, NAZI GERMANY has some lessons to teach us.

I am aware, of course, that parallels between Nazi Germany and the United States can easily be overdrawn, but this danger should not stop us from learning some hard lessons from that dark period when the church struggled to find its identity and had to suffer for what it believed. As you read this book, you might be surprised to see that those similarities are happening before our eyes.

I believe it is disingenuous when political opponents here in the United States call those who disagree with them "Nazis" or "Hitler." The atrocities committed by the Nazis are in a class by themselves; such labels are out of place in our political debate. But I have written this book to show that Nazism did not arise in a vacuum. There were cultural streams that made it possible for this ideology to emerge and gain a wide acceptance by the popular culture. Some of those streams—myths accepted by the masses—are in evidence in America today, and hence this book.

When we think of Nazi Germany, we immediately think of the Holocaust, the brutal murder of millions of Jews and other "undesirables." But we need to realize that there were circumstances and widely accepted ideas that enabled the population to become a part of an evil that was greater than that of any individual. The gas ovens were the end result of certain political and religious trends that made the horrors possible. Read this stinging rebuke from Viktor Frankl, a Holocaust survivor:

> The gas chambers of Auschwitz were the ultimate consequence of the theory that man is nothing but the product of heredity and environment—or as the Nazis liked to say, "Of blood and soil." I'm absolutely convinced that the gas chambers of Auschwitz, Treblinka, and Maidanek were ultimately prepared not in some ministry or other of Berlin, but rather at the desks and in the lecture halls of nihilistic scientists and philosophers.[1]

It is said that after God died in the nineteenth century, man died in the twentieth. For when God is dead, man becomes an untamed beast.

I don't expect that America will ever gas millions of people because they belong to the wrong race; *but the same values that destroyed Germany are being taught in many of our centers of learning today.* Our freedoms are being eroded and, as we shall see, we are being betrayed by the elite—those who should be guarding our liberties are bowing to cultural currents that will, barring a miracle, eventually destroy us.

Those who have read my previous work *Hitler's Cross* know that I undertook a study of Nazi Germany because I often wondered why the pastors of Germany did not condemn Hitler with one unified and courageous voice. I was interested in why the church was seduced by false promises of a great and glorious Germany. *When a Nation Forgets God,* perhaps more than any other book I've written, forces us to grapple with the conflict between our allegiance to government and our greater allegiance to God.

We shall discover that we always find ourselves caught between our responsibility as citizens of earth and our responsibility as citizens of heaven. The church has always been poised between two gods and two crosses. On the one side is our Lord and Savior, Jesus Christ, who died on a Roman cross, executed for the sins of the world. On the other side are any number of lesser gods and other crosses that promise a false salvation. These other gods are almost always embodied in the state; they most often come to us dressed in the garb of Caesar. And in the end they are committed to crushing religious freedom.

Today we face cultural pressures that are forcing us to combine Christ with other religions, or to combine Christ with a political or ideological agenda. The experience of the church in Nazi Germany reminds us that Christ must always stand alone; He must be worshiped not as One who stands alongside the governmental leaders of this world, but as standing above them as *King of kings* and *Lord of lords*.

Whether it's Nazism, Marxism, or Secularism, the state is always in conflict with religious freedom. And the more power the state has, the more laws it will pass to diminish the role of the church. What makes this so difficult is that these changes are made under the rubric of freedom and "what is best for everyone." Thus the true nature of a totalitarian state is always hidden and always couched in the language of morality, progress, and liberty. As in George Orwell's *Animal Farm*, slavery is defined as freedom, and suppression is defined as "the quest for equality and fairness."

Since I believe, as Santayana has said, that those who disregard history are condemned to repeat it, I believe we are derelict if we do not study the Nazi era to learn all we can about our present struggle as the church in America. And, as we shall see, in doing so we might be preparing ourselves for our own impending future.

Back in the 1970s, Francis Schaeffer told us that one day we would wake up and discover that the America we once knew was gone. That day is here. One does not have to be a prophet to see that dark days are coming to the United States. There are ominous signs that the freedoms we once assumed were ours are disappearing. Forces of secularism lead inevitably to a totalitarian state to which everyone is expected to submit.

What are we to do? Wring our hands and wait for the return of Christ? The return of Christ *is* a cherished dream of every Christian, but meanwhile we have a job to do. And rather than fearing what is to come, we need to see the unfolding future as an opportunity to bring glory to God through our steadfast commitment to what will never pass away.

We have the privilege of following in the footsteps of other Christians who have had to put their allegiance to

Christ above their allegiance to the laws of the state. They most assuredly will be rewarded by our Lord Jesus Christ. They did not offer to the Lord that which cost them nothing.

So I invite you to come on a journey to Nazi Germany, and there discover that this is our journey too. A journey that will bring greater understanding and appreciation for our faith in Jesus as King of Kings and Lord of Lords.

This is a journey that invites us to make tough choices for Jesus Christ. It is a journey that forces us to reexamine what we already know to be true!

Chapter One

WHEN GOD IS SEPARATED
FROM GOVERNMENT,
JUDGMENT FOLLOWS

HITLER DID NOT discourage people from attending church. He was a baptized Catholic who had long since abandoned his faith, but he did not mind if others continued to attend church as long as it did not affect the way they lived or the values they held. In fact, he explicitly said that he would not interfere with the specific doctrines of the church, just as long as the churches were teaching those things that were in harmony with the good of the German people. He called this "Positive Christianity."

Of course he knew he would encounter some opposition from those who were not on board with his vision of a toothless Christianity. But he believed that he could crush any opposition he might encounter—and in effect he did just that—by intimidation and controlling their salaries. (Because Germany had a state church, the pastors were dependent on the good graces of the government for their income.) Hitler ridiculed the Protestant pastors, saying they were cowering dogs who would do his bidding for the sake of "their miserable salaries."

So, right from the beginning Hitler sought to marginalize the church to guarantee that no Christian influence would be allowed to inform government policy. Worship would have to be a private matter between a man and his God; at all costs the official state policy would have to be based on humanistic principles to give Hitler the freedom to do what was "best" for Germany. He said that the churches must be "forbidden from interfering with temporal matters." *The state would have to be scrubbed clean of all Christian convictions and values.*

Since Germans had for centuries celebrated Christmas and Easter, Hitler had to reinterpret their meaning. Christmas was turned into a totally pagan festival; in fact, at least for the SS troops, its date was changed to December 21, the date of the winter solstice. School prayers were banned, and carols and Nativity plays were forbidden in the schools; and in 1938 even the name *Christmas* was changed to *Yuletide.* Crucifixes were eliminated from classrooms. Easter was turned into a holiday that heralded the arrival of spring. If religion was tolerated, it had to be secularized so that it would be compatible with the state's commitment to the greater good of a revived Germany. Most of the churches bowed to the cultural currents and endorsed the "Positive Christianity" that was in line with government policies.

Of course, Hitler's real intentions were not immediately revealed. Soon after he was sworn in as chancellor, he paid tribute to Christianity as an "essential element for safeguarding the soul of the German people" and promised to respect the rights of the churches. He declared his ambition to have "a peaceful accord between Church and State."[1] He expressed his intentions to improve his relationship with Pope Pius XII. He also distributed a picture of himself coming out the door of a church to show that he had religious sympathies.

He was willing to give the churches freedom, he said, "as long as they did not do anything subversive to the state." Of course behind that promise lay his own definition of what might be subversive. But this guarded promise, as well as a concordat with the Vatican that appeared to guarantee freedom for the Catholic Church, was welcomed.

Article 24 of the party platform demanded, "liberty for all religious denominations in the State so far as they are not a danger ... to the moral feelings of the German race." Hitler spoke approvingly of his "Positive Christianity" that would contribute to the German struggle. He won some goodwill by appearing to be conciliatory; the churches liked his use of the words *freedom* and *tolerance*. He assured them that he was doing what was best for Germany. Of course, what was "best" would be defined by him, not by the churches, not by the Bible, not even by natural law.

The Germans had become accustomed to the doctrine of the "two spheres," which was interpreted to mean that Christ is Lord of the church, but the Kaiser (or Caesar) is, after a manner of speaking, lord over the political sphere. Allegiance to the political sphere was as high and honorable a duty as was one's allegiance to God. Indeed, allegiance to God was best demonstrated by allegiance to the State.

Within the Lutheran church there was a strong pietistic

movement that advocated a return to biblical piety, the worship of God within the heart. For the most part these people were opposed to biblical scholarship (especially of the liberal kind) and withdrew from the intellectual theological debates within Germany. They witnessed to the saving grace of Christ but believed that the church's mission was only to preach Christ. Pietism, with its emphasis on personal devotion to Christ, was used to inject spiritual life into the mainstream Lutheran church. But by insisting that that their faith was private and should not be brought into the political sphere, pietism had scant influence in stemming the Nazi tide.

So those who dutifully tolerated the excesses of the Nazi regime, but simply continued to study the Bible to maintain a warm heart, are to be commended for getting it half right. Certainly they were much more effective than those who ceased to study their Bibles and enthusiastically endorsed the regime. These pious Christians thought that if they left Hitler alone, he would leave them alone. But they discovered that was not possible. Hitler also put pressure on them to have their children indoctrinated in the state schools and, thanks to the cultural pressure, their churches were not equipping members to stand against the abuses that were developing around them.

USING THE CHURCH

Before Hitler moved to destroy the church, he decided to make peace with it and use it for his own ends. On March 21, 1933, he arranged an impressive spectacle for the opening of the new session of the Reichstag (German Parliament) in the

Garrison Church in Potsdam. With pomp and ceremony he sought to assure the nation that he could follow a conservative path and seek harmony with the churches. Two days after the ceremony, the Reichstag passed the so-called Enabling Law whereby the power of the Reichstag was reduced to a sounding board for the party. The necessary majority to pass the bill was secured by the arrest of some opposition parliament members and the threatening of others. By July, Hitler proclaimed the Nazis as the only party in Germany.

Despite his conciliatory beginning, Hitler would later try to obliterate the church. In the end, he wanted to transform the church so thoroughly that every vestige of Christianity would be smashed. There was not enough room in the churches for both the cross and the swastika. As he himself mused, "One god must dominate another." Given the weaknesses of the church, his goal appeared to be within reach, though it would not be as easy as he thought.

NIEMOLLER MEETS HITLER

Martin Niemoller and Dietrich Bonhoeffer (we shall meet both of these men in more detail later in this book) gathered opposition to Hitler's intrusion into the affairs of the church. When Hitler heard that there might be a church split because some pastors objected to his agenda, he summoned the leaders of the churches to a personal conference to which Niemoller was included on January 25, 1934. Niemoller and other members of the clergy walked past the SS guards to the Reich Chancellery in Berlin and soon were ushered into Hitler's study.

Hitler began by reproaching his guests, treating them to a tirade about how he was misunderstood. "Peace," he said, is all that he wanted. "Peace between Church and state." He blamed them for obstructing him, sabotaging his efforts to achieve it.

"YOU CONFINE YOURSELF TO THE CHURCH. I'LL TAKE CARE OF THE GERMAN PEOPLE."

—HITLER

Niemoller was waiting for a chance to speak, and when he had the opportunity, explained that his only object was the welfare of the church, the state, and the German people. Hitler listened in silence and then said, "You confine yourself to the Church. I'll take care of the German people." The conversation then drifted to other themes.

When it was over, Hitler shook hands with the clergy and Niemoller realized this would be his last opportunity to speak his mind. Carefully choosing his words, he said, "You said that 'I will take care of the German people.' But we too, as Christians and churchmen, have a responsibility toward the German people. That responsibility was entrusted to us by God, and neither you nor anyone in this world has the power to take it from us."[2] Hitler turned away without a word.

That same evening, eight Gestapo men ransacked Niemoller's rectory for incriminating material. A few days later a homemade bomb exploded in the hall. Interestingly, the police came to the scene even though no one had called them. These threats were easier for Niemoller to bear than some of the criticism he received from his colleagues for his strong words to Hitler. Clearly the majority of the clergy had adopted an attitude of safety first. More than two thousand pastors who had stood with Niemoller and Bonhoeffer withdrew their support. They believed that appeasement was the best strategy; they thought that if they remained silent they could live with Hitler's intrusion into church affairs and his political policies.

PUT YOURSELF IN THEIR SHOES
AND ASK: "WHAT WOULD *I* HAVE DONE?"

Please read this eyewitness account of how some members of the church reacted to the Nazism of their times. Put yourself in their shoes and ask: "What would *I* have done?"

I lived in Germany during the Nazi Holocaust. I considered myself a Christian. We heard stories of what was happening to the Jews, but we tried to distance ourselves from it, because, what could anyone do to stop it?

A railroad track ran behind our small church and each Sunday morning we could hear the whistle in the distance and then the wheels coming over the tracks. We became disturbed when we heard the cries coming from the train as it passed by. We realized that it was carrying Jews like cattle in the cars!

Week after week the whistle would blow. We dreaded to hear the sound of those wheels because we knew that we would hear the cries of the Jews en route to a death camp. Their screams tormented us.

We knew the time the train was coming and when we heard the whistle blow we began singing hymns. By the time the train came past our church we were singing at the top of our voices. If we heard the screams, we sang more loudly and soon we heard them no more.

Years have passed and no one talks about it anymore. But I still hear that train whistle in my sleep. God forgive me; forgive all of us who called ourselves Christians yet did nothing to intervene.[3]

We should not be too critical of the church in Germany. What would we have done in the face of such abuses? What should we do when the state's policy is evil? What train is rumbling past us today whose whistle we ignore? Answers are not easy to come by. Yet the question is just as relevant today as it was back then: *What is the role of the church in the face of governments that have self-consciously excluded God from their policies?* Was Hitler right when he told Niemoller that he should limit himself to taking care of the church while he (Hitler) had the responsibility of taking care of the German people? Or was Niemoller right in insisting that the church also had responsibility for the German people at large?

Hitler responded to the opposition of the church in the same way all hostile governments respond to those who would disagree with them: He created a flurry of new laws and then accused pastors and church leaders of breaking them. In one way or another God had to be separated from government policies and ejected from the public square. The voice of courageous Christians had to be silenced. *God had to be removed to make way for the National Socialist policies.*

Niemoller was later imprisoned for what we today call "hate speech" because he dared criticize the regime within his church. Specifically, the charges against him were "abuse of pulpit" and he was charged with speaking "with malicious and provocative criticism . . . of a kind calculated to undermine the confidence of the People in their political leaders." He had involved himself with matters that "were of concern only to the state."[4] He had violated a new law for the "Prevention of Treacherous Attacks on State and Party." For speaking out—his crime was simply preaching what he believed his people should hear—he was sentenced to prison and then confined to concentration camps, ending up in Dachau where he remained until liberated by Allied troops.

Hitler always said that the best way to conquer your enemies is to divide them. He encouraged a movement simply called "God Believers" (he was willing to use the word *God* as long as it was emptied of all essential meaning), a policy designed to persuade individuals to withdraw from the churches. The sales pitch was that there was an alternative to the church; the state could have a ceremony to dedicate infants; the state could have its own holidays without the need to celebrate the Christian ones. Marriages, for those who wished, could also be performed by the state. The blessings of Mother Earth and Father Sky were frequently invoked upon the couple until their destiny was fulfilled. In the same way, same-sex marriage proponents say today that marriage can take place without the blessings of a religious body; it can be a purely secular act separated from religious overtones.

And so it was that secularism was imposed on the German people. The role of the church was minimized by privatizing faith and instituting laws about what could or could not be said from a pulpit. Religious leaders who opposed the secular steamroller were intimidated by threats to them and their families. With God and religion removed from government, the values of Hitler's socialism filled the vacuum. The church would increasingly become the enemy of the state.

Keep in mind that all of this happened under code words such as *freedom, peace,* and *fairness.* The people were assured that these changes were made with their best interests in mind. The Greater Good of Germany eclipsed individual freedoms and the right to opposition. Everyone was expected to be in sync with the accepted cultural values and goals. Those who opposed the regime paid a price.

WHITHER AMERICA?

Here in America where freedom of speech is expressly granted in the Constitution, we might think that Nazi Germany has little to teach us about a secular state. If you think that is the case, think again. When truth is rejected in the public sphere, the state will either turn to some semblance of natural law or more ominously, to lies. Secular values will be imposed on society, and it will be done in the name of "freedom."

Our social planners who are dedicated to reshaping America according to purely humanistic values agree with Hitler that God and religion must be removed from government. The American Civil Liberties Union (ACLU) believes that God must be separated not just from government, but from every sphere of American life. Religion—particularly Christianity—must be ousted from government, from law, education, and the workplace.[5]

Thus with the so-called public square free of any hint of religious values, the vacuum is then filled with secular values: the cheapness of human life (abortion and euthanasia), the promotion of all forms of immorality (including homosexual marriages), and the sexualization of schoolchildren (often with pornography and the ridicule of traditional values). This secularism is not religiously neutral but is being imposed upon society as the only viable point of view. So, laws are being passed that will prevent effective opposition to these changes, so that secularism can reign supreme. Freedoms formerly a part of our history can be withdrawn as religion is designated as "private," which is code for "irrelevant" and "powerless."

Just as Germany had Christian holidays paganized, just so, we have witnessed the systematic removal of religious symbols from public places. First it was crosses on Christmas trees, and then it was Christmas trees themselves that became a point of controversy. During the holiday season public schools seldom refer to Christmas anymore in their celebrations. Instead, they use phrases such as "winter program" or "winter holidays." Following a school board decision to rename a school's Christmas program a "winter" program, teachers in one district even began to forbid their students to say the word *Christmas* on school grounds.[6] The ACLU stands ready to intimidate any teacher who dares to tell students that Christmas is a religious holiday. A kindergartener asking God's blessing on her lunch was tapped on the shoulder by her teacher and was told that she must not do that at school.[7] All this, despite the fact that compelling arguments can be made that America's prosperity, freedoms, and generosity can be traced to its founding as a nation rooted in faith in God and respect for the Bible as His Word.

SHE REPLIED, "THE PEOPLE IN CHINA HAVE FREEDOM OF RELIGION . . . THEY CAN BE AS FREE AS THEY WISH WITHIN THEIR OWN MINDS!"

When my family and I were in the People's Republic of China back in 1985, we asked a tour guide about freedom of religion. She replied, "The people in China have freedom of religion . . . they can be as free as they wish within their own minds!" Freedom of religion, then, has a new definition: We are free to practice our religion with our thoughts and perhaps in private conversation. In our own country one of our chief justices lamented that the court would have religion be like "pornography," indulged only in private.[8]

When God is ousted from government, transcendent values are replaced by:

- The raw use of power
- Eroticism
- Arbitrary judicial rulings
- The morality of personal pragmatism

Without overarching absolutes, the unity of society is threatened in the face of fragmentation and the quest for personal "rights." Civility, long a characteristic of American life, has degenerated into name-calling and a desire to destroy the opposition. As Dostoyevsky has famously said, when God does not exist, anything is possible.

Political correctness has now affected the general culture and created an aura of censorship and a climate of fear. Many years ago Malcolm Muggeridge said, "The whole structure is now tumbling down, dethroning its God, undermining all its certainties. All this, wonderfully enough, is being done in the name of the health, wealth, and happiness of all mankind."[9] As John Whitehead says, "The noose is growing tighter around religious speech and its various expressions."[10] And, yes, Muggeridge is right, this is all being done in the name of health, wealth, and the happiness (and we might add the *equality*) of all mankind!

Several years ago, hate crimes legislation was passed in both the US Senate and the House of Representatives. Although the Senate version contained an exemption for religious institutions, the language of this special exemption was somewhat weakened when reconciled with the version passed by the House. The bottom line is that we are going down a dangerous path as "hate crimes" are linked to "hate speech" and thus our First Amendment rights are curtailed. Thus, certain classes of people receive special treatment under the law. From "Hate *Crimes*" the next step is for the courts to prosecute those who are deemed guilty of "Hate *Speech*," which one of our senators called "domestic terrorism." Thus, what we think and what we say are both open to prosecution. Hate speech in this country will mean the same as it did in Nazi Germany: *It is simply stating an opinion that the government thinks should not be expressed.*

No wonder the Muslim community supports hate-speech legislation. Britons are hotly debating issues of "hate speech" against Muslims. For the most part, Europe has already lost the freedom to criticize Islam. Given the strong response to the cartoon controversy of a few years ago (when more than a hundred people died in riots), and given laws against hate speech, the Europeans are paralyzed, incapable of speaking their mind even on subjects that are important to their future. We shall return to this subject in a later chapter.

More than a decade ago, John Whitehead, speaking of America, observed, "Citizens increasingly feel powerless to act. Indeed, modern governments often pose a threat more serious than the older ones because government has become even more pervasive. The modern welfare state controls more and more of the totality of life—often in response to the demands of its citizens that it do so."[11] If that was true a decade ago, think of how much more relevant it is today.

As the state encroaches on our liberties, the spiritual

"sphere" will continue to shrink, and our freedoms will be slowly curtailed. Statism, the notion that there is no power above the state to which it must be subject, will always work toward the diminishing of individual freedoms. No one is able to run and hide. "Statism," someone has said, "is the Golden Calf of the modern world."

OUR CHILLING FUTURE

What can we expect in the future?

Here in America there will probably be no overnight revolution culminating in totalitarianism, but as Whitehead predicts, "Rather, the current trend of government, media and public state-controlled education toward greater control and manipulation of the individual citizen will continue."[12] Today our government has tools of manipulation that the world has never known before, from mass communication resources to faceless computerized bureaucracies to the ability to nationalize banks and companies.

And as Whitehead writes, "The media does more than affect public opinion—*it alters the consciences and worldview of entire generations.*"[13] All of this will be imposed upon us with the reminder that this is for our good, that it benefits the majority, that it is for the sake of "freedom" and "fairness" and, of course, "tolerance." C. S. Lewis was a prophet when he wrote:

> Of all tyrannies, a tyranny sincerely exercised for the good of its victims may be the most oppressive.... Those who torment us for our own good will torment us without end for

they do so with the approval of their own conscience. . . . In reality, however, we must face the possibility of bad rulers armed with a Humanitarian theory of punishment. . . . We know that one school of psychology already regards religion as a neurosis. When this particular neurosis becomes inconvenient to government, what is to hinder government from proceeding to "cure" it? Such a "cure" will, of course, be compulsory; but under the Humanitarian theory it will not be called by the shocking name of Persecution.[14]

WHEN DO WE TOLERATE THE CURTAILMENT OF OUR FREEDOMS AND AT WHAT POINT SHOULD WE SPEAK AND ACT?

A while back I read the headline, "Florida Principal, Athletic Director Could Go to Jail for Prayer Before Lunch at School."

The text reads, "A principal and an athletic director could be charged with crimes and spend six months in jail after they prayed before a meal at a school event, the *Washington Times* reported. . . . They're accused of violating the conditions of a lawsuit settlement reached last year with the American Civil Liberties Union, according to the *Times*."[15]

We can expect more such headlines in the future. As Americans we must keep in mind that the First Amendment was not intended to mean that atheists and agnostics have veto power over all those who believe in God.[16] We need to develop a "theology of civil disobedience"; that is, we need to think through this question: When do we tolerate the curtailment of our freedoms and at what point should we speak and act? That, of course, is beyond the scope of this book. But we are not left without guidance, for men like Niemoller have shown us the way.

FROM NIEMOLLER'S HEART

Niemoller has a word for us who live in America. Of course he was thinking of his own church and the people of Germany when he spoke these words, but they are for us as well. Early in 1934, he mounted the pulpit of his church in the Berlin suburb of Dahlem and prophetically declared God's purpose in the trials that faced the German church:

> We have all of us—the whole Church and the whole community—we've been thrown into the Tempter's sieve, and he is shaking and the wind is blowing, and it must now become manifest whether we are wheat or chaff! Verily, a time of sifting has come upon us, and even the most indolent and peaceful person among us must see that the calm of a meditative Christianity is at an end. . . .
>
> It is now springtime for the hopeful and expectant Christian Church—it is testing time, and God is giving Satan a free hand, so he may shake us up and so that it may be seen what manner of men we are! . . .
>
> Satan swings his sieve and Christianity is thrown hither

and thither; and he who is not ready to suffer, he who called himself a Christian only because he thereby hoped to gain something good for his race and his nation is blown away like chaff by the wind of time.[17]

Yes, God is separating the wheat and the chaff! This is no time to pout but to accept our role as Christians in this society with joy. Yes, with every challenge to our liberties we have another opportunity to prove our love for Christ and the gospel. Bonheoffer was right when he said that we will never be a victorious church until we see suffering as a divine *gift*. "For to you it has been granted on behalf of Christ, not only to believe in Him but to suffer for his sake" (Philippians 1:29 NKJV). God sends persecution to both purify her and to sharpen her Christian witness.

It is time for us to reread the New Testament book of 1 Peter, written specifically to believers living in a hostile, pagan culture. They had no representatives in government to plead their case; they had no power to "vote the bums out" as we do in America. They did not have courts that would give them a fair hearing. There was just persecution, intimidation, and deprivation. And sometimes death.

To them Peter wrote, "Dear friends, do not be surprised at the painful trial you are suffering, as though something strange were happening to you. But rejoice that you participate in the sufferings of Christ, so that you may be overjoyed when his glory is revealed. If you are insulted because of the name of Christ, you are blessed, for the Spirit of glory and of God rests on you" (1 Peter 4:12–14 NIV).

WE WILL NOT WIN THESE BATTLES SIMPLY WITH POLITICS (HOWEVER IMPORTANT THAT IS) NOR BY ARGUMENT.

When confronted with these challenges we are tempted to do the wrong thing—to react with judgmental anger that will only entrench those who are on the other side in this culture war. We must do the opposite: to respond with humility, love, and gracious courage. We will neither win these battles simply with politics (however important that is) nor by argument. Every Christian must regain the high ground with credibility, winsomeness, and yes, with joy. We must stand our ground giving thanks to God, even as it shifts beneath our feet. *We dare not give to Caesar that which is God's.*

Niemoller was right: we are being sifted to separate the wheat and the chaff. Whether in Nazi Germany or America, believers cannot choose to remain silent under the guise of preaching the gospel. Sharing the gospel is, of course, our primary responsibility since it is only the cross of Christ that can transform the human heart. But once we have received the gift of salvation through Christ, we must live out the implications of the cross in every area of our life. We must be prepared to submit to the Lordship of Christ in all "spheres."

Here in America we must respond to our own challenges on multiple levels. We must educate our citizenry on both our history and what is taking place in our government, courts, and schools. We must do our homework in knowing what our politicians believe about these issues and be sure to vote for those who are most compatible with our values.

Then we must also support organizations that are working to preserve our freedoms, such as the National Religious Broadcasters in Washington (www.nrb.org), which is dedicated to keeping media outlets free of government interference for the proclamation of the gospel.

Finally, we must strengthen individual believers in our churches for the ominous days ahead. As I've already mentioned, the future of America will ultimately rest, not on politicians, but on the fervency of God's people in sharing their faith as credible witnesses to the Christ who saved them. Unless the culture changes, America will not change. And that change is best brought about one life, one family, and one community at a time.

Keep reading.

Chapter Two

IT'S ALWAYS
THE ECONOMY

IMAGINE THIS SCENARIO: Inflation is out of control; the price of bread, milk, and vegetables (when available) runs into the thousands of dollars. Candles and combustible household furnishings are replacing heat and electricity as public utilities are closed due to unattainable wage and labor demands. And these "demands" arise from an inflationary cycle fueled by fear and frustration; unemployment numbers continue to rise daily at frightening speed.

Disease runs rampant. Hospitals are not only closed but also abandoned; medicine (or whatever of it remains) is being hoarded by the privileged few or traded in bartered transactions. The rich hide behind their gated communities and vigilante groups are formed to protect the "haves" from the "have-nots" who are roaming the streets destroying property, killing randomly, and stealing. With a porous border, drug lords come from Mexico to wreak destruction and find what they can steal amid the chaos.

Nearly all public services such as schools, police, fire, and emergency networks have likewise been discontinued as the infrastructure of a civilized society rapidly disintegrates. Even the remnant of a federal militia cannot enforce martial law. Thus, chaos and crime explode on the scene as families and family units implode. Relatives huddle together trying to survive and those who have friends or relatives outside of the big cities, flee hoping to save their lives and sanity.

People are indeed angry . . . very angry. And that anger is primarily directed at the government—a government that promised not only life, liberty, and the pursuit of happiness but stability, and even prosperity. People are angry when they realize that their government is hopelessly indebted to foreign countries; multiple billions of dollars were borrowed as though they did not have to be repaid. The billions owed have become trillions and the day of reckoning has come.

Hostile crowds demand that banks allow them to withdraw their funds in cash, but of course, the banks have long since run out of hard currency, even though the dollar is devalued almost weekly if not daily. People are demanding action; the populace feels betrayed. Even when the president speaks, few hear him, for electronic communication is unreliable. Even so, those who do hear him disbelieve what he says. And why should they trust his words? . . . The promise has become a lie.

I'm sure that the populace at large—including all of us today in twenty-first-century America—would be willing to tolerate the suspension of such civil liberties as freedom of speech, freedom of assembly, and freedom of worship—and even the freedom of free elections—in exchange for stability and order. People would submit to rations, travel restrictions, and a ban on demonstrations. We'd trade our freedoms for one gift: the gift of survival. If a dictator arose who gave credible evidence that he could bring order out of the chaos, we'd be willing to let him have whatever power and freedom he needed.

Let us not be quick to condemn those who were willing to give Hitler a chance, given the economic chaos that spread through Germany after World War I. He could never have come to power if the German economy would have remained strong after World War I. He rode to victory simply because he promised to rebuild the collapsing German mark and put the nation back to work. He cleverly exploited the economic crisis that postwar Germany was experiencing. Yes, it was the economy that gave rise to National Socialism.

Germany's inflation was triggered by a huge increase in the nation's money supply because of the heavy reparations assigned to Germany after losing World War I. The German government chose to pay its debts with cheap marks, printing as many as needed to stem the crisis. When the initial injections of newly printed money failed to work, the government's response was more of the same. The result was to print still more.

Economists are agreed that "hyperinflation" is brought about by an unchecked increase in the money supply, usually accompanied by a widespread unwillingness on the part of the people to hold the money for more than the time needed to trade it for something tangible to avoid further loss. Hyperinflation is usually associated with wars, economic depressions, and political and social upheavals. It is associated with governments that artificially create wealth to extend the benefits of the state to a populace in crisis.

Stories of what life was like in postwar Germany abound. People who had fixed incomes were wiped out financially. Retirement funds were reduced to zero. Prices changed by the hour. It is said that a student at Freiburg University ordered a cup of coffee for 5,000 marks. He decided to order a second cup. When his bill was 14,000 marks he protested but was told, "If you want to save money and you want two cups of coffee, you should order both of them at the same time."

There is a story, perhaps fictitious, of a woman who filled her wheelbarrow with German marks and left them outside the store, confident that no one would bother stealing the money. Sure enough, when it was time to pay for her groceries, she walked outside only to discover that the bundles of money were left on the ground but the wheelbarrow was gone! We might smile at the story, but for the Germans there was nothing to smile about. Their savings were totally wiped out. They had lost faith in their government. The people suffered immeasurably, and the worst was yet to come.

However—and this is important—there were benefits to this runaway inflation. Businesses with significant debt were glad when the value of the mark fell so that they could repay their loans with essentially worthless pieces of paper. In fact, big industrialists and landlords goaded the government into deliberately letting the mark tumble in order to free the State of its public commitments and assist businesses that needed to erase their large debts. The masses suffered, of course, because their savings disappeared when the mark was devalued. When 1,000-billion notes were printed, few bothered to collect the change when they spent it. By November 1923, with one dollar equal to a trillion marks, the breakdown was complete. Unused marks were used to light fires.

Predictably, anarchy erupted, particularly in the big cities. Gasoline was siphoned from cars; whatever was not nailed down was stolen and whatever could be bartered was used in exchange for food or clothes. In the midst of the chaos, the government was forced to leave Berlin and move to the National Theatre in Weimar to attempt to form a new government based on democratic principles and ideals.

AT THE HEIGHT OF THE INFLATIONARY CYCLE, THE PEOPLE CRIED OUT FOR SOMEONE TO END THE MADNESS.

At the height of the continuing inflationary cycle, the people cried out for someone to end the madness. Even when the mark was in a free fall, the government would not stop printing money, because it saw no way out of the chaos. So the people longed for a strong leader—a dictator who would be able to put an end to the charade and have a new beginning with a new currency, and with it institute the controls that a stable economy would need. And there was just such a man waiting for this moment.

An economic crisis is always a gift to a leader who wants

to capture a nation. And Hitler was delirious with joy over his country's economic ills. Inflation and unemployment was the disease for which he had the cure. He did not want to let this financial crisis go to waste.

THE ARRIVAL OF HITLER

Hitler holds a fascination for us because his dictatorship enjoyed such wide support of the people. Perhaps never in history was a dictator so well liked. He had the rare gift of motivating a nation to want to follow him. Communist leaders such as Lenin or Mao rose to power through revolutions that cost millions of lives; consequently they were hated by the masses. Hitler not only attracted the support of the middle class, but also of university students and professors. For example, the psychologist Carl Jung grew intoxicated with "the mighty phenomenon of National Socialism at which the whole world gazes in astonishment."

In 1923, Hitler's dramatic attempt to overthrow the Bavarian government failed. He had tried to foment a political revolution in Munich that was aborted by the police, and sixteen of his men were killed. He was convicted of treason; and after his stay in the Landsberg Prison, he decided to gain power through the political process. He would use democracy as the path to power and then crush it once he gained control. Democracy was the stepping-stone to dictatorship.

The economic outlook improved in 1925–29 with unemployment down and retail sales up. Ten years after the war ended, the German Republic seemed to come into its own. The Nazi Party was all but dead. But Hitler, with the passion of world conquest burning in his breast, simply would not give up. He kept waiting, hoping that Germany would experience bad times.

The worldwide depression of 1929 gave Hitler the opportunity he sought. Revolutionary that he was, he could thrive only in bad times when unemployment was high, inflation was rampant, and anger and mistrust spread throughout Germany. This was his time to capture the nation, not by war but by constitutional means.

When Austria's biggest bank collapsed, it forced the banks in Berlin to close temporarily. Germany was unable to make its war payments; millions were unemployed as thousands of small businesses were wiped out. Deprived of jobs and a decent living, and ravaged by hunger, the Germans were willing to do anything to survive.

For Hitler these were fertile times to gain the ear and vote of the masses. Anticipating an election in March 1933 that he knew he could not win, he chose to create a crisis. On February 27, 1933, the Reichstag building in Berlin was in flames. The evidence points to arson, most probably that Hitler's men forced a Dutchman named Marinus van der Lubbe to enter the building through a passage used for the heating system. At gunpoint, he set a fire in the basement of the building and soon the massive structure was in flames.

Hitler blamed the arson on a communist conspiracy and induced Paul von Hindenburg (the aged German president) to sign a decree "for the protection of the people and the state" that suspended individual liberties. The Nazis could search homes without a warrant, confiscate property, and outlaw the meetings of groups that might oppose them.

Interestingly, von Hindenburg was acting in accordance with the Weimar Constitution, which stipulated that the president could bypass Parliament in the event of an emergency!

Though Hitler still failed to get a majority, by murder, threats, and promises, he did manage to get a two-thirds majority vote in the Reichstag to amend the constitution. By this amendment, all legislative functions were granted to the Reich Cabinet, which transferred these powers to Hitler personally. From now on, he, not the Reichstag, would make the laws. On July 14, he decreed that the Nazis would be the sole political party in Germany.

His report card is filled with such astounding achievements that many Christians saw him as an answer to their prayers. Some Christians, I have been told—yes, I said *Christians*—took a picture of Christ from the wall in their homes and substituted a portrait of Hitler. Winston Churchill observed Hitler in 1937 and said that his accomplishments were "among the most remarkable in the whole history of the world."

Hitler's brand of socialism had many advantages for the German people. By nationalizing the banks, instituting wage and price controls, and centralizing the economy, National Socialism could bypass the often-slow democratic process and get things done quickly. Despite Hitler's gross crimes, he did have an economic policy that appeared to work, at least for the first few years. Here is his outstanding report card:

1. He revived a collapsed economy in four years.
2. He instituted nationalized health care.
3. He gave millions of Germans attractive vacations

through his *Kraft durch Freude* ("Strength through Joy") program.

4. He established training schools for those who were unskilled and brought the nation to full employment.
5. He brought crime under control.
6. He instituted a huge public works program and built freeways and promised the production of a car that ordinary Germans would soon be able to afford.
7. He gave Germans a reason to believe in themselves, to believe that they could become great again.

If only he had died before World War II, one historian mused, he would have gone down in history as "Adolf the Great, one of the outstanding figures in German history."

But Hitler didn't die before World War II; he didn't die until the German people had surrendered their personal rights; he didn't die until laws were enacted that led to the extermination of more than eight million people, and until Germany and several other countries were destroyed in a war that killed fifty million people in the greatest bloodbath in history. He didn't die until thousands of pastors joined the SS troops in swearing personal allegiance to him. What began as an economic miracle ended with a moral and political nightmare.

THE POWER OF THE ECONOMY

By and large the Germans offered little resistance to National Socialism because they saw its obvious benefits.

Listen to what Gerald Suster writes: "Many welcomed the abolition of individual responsibility for one's actions; for some it is easier to obey than to accept the dangers of freedom. Workers now had job security, a health service, cheap holiday schemes; if freedom meant starvation, then slavery was preferable."[1] The man for whom they had waited had arrived.

As long as the economy was strong, people didn't care whether they had freedom of speech, freedom of travel, or freedom of elections. Under the Republic, people were starving in the big cities; they agreed that bread on the table was more important than a ballot at a voting booth. The people were willing to forgive Hitler's purges and his ruthless massacres in return for the right to live.

By far the majority of the Lutheran churches sided with Hitler and his spectacular reforms. But a minority, under the leadership of Bonhoeffer and Niemoller, chose to pull away from the established church to form the "Confessing Church." This breakaway church that opposed Hitler held its own synods and wrote its own protests to the continued intrusion of Nazism into the life of the church. In 1938, when the German pastors were mandated to swear personal allegiance to Hitler, the synod essentially "wimped out" and refused to take a stand against the political firestorm that now engulfed them.

The synod did that which could only gladden the heart of Hitler himself: they decided that individual pastors and church leaders should make up their own minds about signing the Aryan clause and taking the oath of loyalty. This made it easy for the Gestapo to identify any pastor who didn't comply, arrest him, and sentence him to whatever the "People's Court" would decide.

As a result, about eight hundred pastors were arrested and imprisoned.

THE RESPONSE OF THE PEOPLE

What did the rest of Germany think of the news that eight hundred pastors were imprisoned for not accepting the Nazification of their churches? We are shocked at the indifference of the German populace in the face of such abuses. William Shirer, in his monumental *The Rise and Fall of the Third Reich*, gives one of the most chilling assessments of the values that the Germans held dear. Though this paragraph is long, I encourage you to read every word. Shirer writes:

It would be misleading to give the impression that the persecution of Protestants and Catholics by the Nazi State tore the German people asunder or even greatly aroused the vast majority of them. It did not. A people who had so lightly given up their political and cultural and economic freedoms were not, except for a relatively few, going to die or even risk imprisonment to preserve freedom of worship. *What really aroused the Germans in the Thirties were the glittering successes of Hitler in providing jobs, creating prosperity, restoring Germany's military might, and moving from one triumph to another in his foreign policy.* Not many Germans lost much sleep over the arrests of a few thousand pastors and priests or over the quarreling of the various Protestant sects. And even fewer paused to reflect that under the leadership of Rosenberg,

Bormann and Himmler, who were backed by Hitler, the Nazi regime intended eventually to destroy Christianity in Germany, if it could, and substitute the old paganism of the early tribal Germanic gods and the new paganism of the Nazi extremists. As Bormann, one of the men closest to Hitler, said publicly in 1941, "National Socialism and Christianity are irreconcilable" (italics added).[2]

So there you have it—the majority of the people, including the Christians in the Third Reich, no longer believed that Christianity was worth suffering for, much less dying for. They were willing to substitute *Mein Kampf* for the Bible in exchange for jobs and the greater glory of Germany. Yet those who saved their lives lost them, and those who lost their lives saved them.

GIVEN A CHOICE, MOST PEOPLE PROBABLY WILL CHOOSE BREAD AND SAUSAGE ABOVE INDIVIDUAL LIBERTIES.

Jobs! Economic security! Prosperity! Most people are willing to close their eyes to glaring warning signs in exchange for a strong economy and money in the bank. Like the late Francis Schaeffer used to tell us, people are willing to march down the wrong path if only they can be assured of personal peace and affluence. They willingly march forward, not asking where that path will lead.

After the fall of the Berlin Wall a cartoon appeared in a Russian newspaper picturing a fork in the road. One path was labeled *freedom*; the other path was labeled *sausage*. As we might guess, the path to freedom had few takers; the path to sausage was crowded with footprints. When given a choice, most people probably will choose bread and sausage above the free market and individual liberties. It was Lenin's promise of bread in every kitchen that ignited the communist revolution. Bread with political slavery was better than freedom and starvation. Bread fills the stomach, freedom does not.

Thanks to the wars he began, Hitler soon had huge deficits and so the German government again printed money to pay for the national debt. Inflation surfaced again and the German people faced another economic crisis after World War II was over. As always, it was the economy that became the number one concern on the minds of the disillusioned German people.

A LESSON FOR THE UNITED STATES

"It's the economy, stupid!"

This was a slogan effectively used here in the United States during the 1992 presidential campaign. People tend to vote their pocketbooks, and while that in itself is not wrong, it can lead to warped values and in some instances the curtailment of freedoms. Money, which is so essential for us to live, can also be the lure that makes us willing to sell our souls.

Of course the United States is not Germany, and, as we have observed, parallels between us and the Nazi era can easily be overdrawn. But there is this abiding lesson: Satan was right when he said, "All that a man has he will give for his life" (Job 2:4). Survival is a powerful drive within us all, and most of us are willing to compromise our values in order to live. And if the government can guarantee our financial future, we support that government even if we intuitively suspect we are being led down a dangerous path. Benjamin Franklin is quoted as saying, "Any society that would give up a little liberty to gain a little security will deserve neither and lose both."

Before I proceed any further, I wish to make one thing clear: *The Bible does not specify which type of economic theory should be adopted by governments.* I am not qualified to comment on what theory of economics would be best for America. However, there are several biblical principles that I think should apply.

First, the personal warnings against debt in the Scriptures could wisely be expanded to include the governments of this world—it is certainly wrong for us to spend our children's money. Thomas Jefferson was right when he said, "The principle of spending money to be paid by posterity, under the name of funding, is but swindling futurity on a large scale."[3] And yet because governments are rewarded for spending and punished for cutting back, it is almost as if our leaders are swiping our personal credit cards to get votes.

Incredibly, we who are known as the wealthiest country on earth have borrowed billions of dollars from other countries—especially China. We might think we should be lend-ing, not borrowing. Listen to what God said to Israel, "For the Lord your God will bless you, as he promised you, and *you shall lend to many nations, but you shall not borrow,* and you shall rule over many nations, but they shall not rule over you" (Deuteronomy 15:6, italics added). We are debtors because as a nation we have refused to live within our means and have borrowed from future generations. Payday is coming.

Second, the biblical warnings against bribes should also be applied to government—it is wrong for politicians to use our money to reward their supporters.

And third, stealing—even if it is from the rich—should be forbidden as a government policy. Yes, much can be said for the graduated income tax scale, but even that can be unfairly used to "equalize" everyone.

I believe that Alexis de Tocqueville was right when he predicted that democracy would not survive if people realized that they could vote themselves money. But politicians know that many people become loyal to any politician who will indeed promise them the most benefits. To vote for the candidate who promised you the most money is stealing (since your entitlement is actually someone else's money). It might be legalized stealing but it is stealing nonetheless.

Without getting into details, my point in this chapter is to simply argue that the economy often trumps matters of liberty and principle because money is so integral to who we are; and, of course, we need money to live. Unfortunately, sometimes it also trumps those values that are eternally important, such as one's honor and witness for the gospel.

Given our penchant for wanting to live and not suffer

deprivation, we are prone to do exactly what the German people did, and that is to overlook eternal ideals for the sake of temporal survival. So often even we as Christians have been willing to compromise Christ to keep our jobs and to be assured of economic security, and to hide our faith in order to graduate from our favorite university.

TWO IMPORTANT LESSONS

We can learn from history that politicians often use an economic crisis to make their subjects more government dependent, and with that dependency comes more control. A few years ago, our government made massive bailout funds available to banks and leading companies that were on the verge of bankruptcy. When our government gave billions to General Motors, as a prerequisite to this help, our president requested that the CEO of the company be relieved of his position even if he was not guilty of wrongdoing. My central point is that the more government dependency, the more government control.

Because a bureaucracy feeds on itself, the government (which is accountable only to itself) is notoriously inefficient in running its affairs. The examples of government waste are legion. Various levels of faceless bureaucracy are formed that stifle creativity and free enterprise. For example, I spoke to a man who was responsible for the distribution of government money to humanitarian projects in different parts of the world. He told me that only 20 percent of the funds actually gets to the people.

The matter of a nationalized health care program in the

United States was hotly debated a few years ago, with some compelling arguments on both sides. I do not minimize the difficulty of balancing all of the relevant data, and the effects of the Affordable Care Act are still unfolding. However, in the British version of national health care, people receive minimum treatment, and those over the age of sixty are routinely denied heart surgery, because at that age such procedures are not "cost effective."[4]

As might be expected, Hitler took the rationing of heath care to the extreme and eliminated those who were no longer worthy of the state-funded benefits. In what is called his T-4 bill, Hitler stipulated that elderly people with an incurable disease and young children who were disabled should be euthanized. Obviously we are not there yet, but—I can already hear it argued—in the interest of fairness would it not make sense to simply put the elderly to sleep to make way for a younger generation at a time when funds are scarce?

A second lesson: With expanded government control comes loss of liberty, and a loss of the work ethic. This was most clearly seen in communist countries where wages were both set by the government and doled out by the government. For the politicians to control the state coffers is of great personal benefit to them, because the more people are dependent on the government for their existence, the more willing they are to bow to whatever the government demands. For many years our government has printed billions of dollars even though we have absolutely no collateral to support it. It is axiomatic that money is power and those in power want more money. And you can be sure that *control follows the money.*

There are two ways to understand the meaning of the word *equality*. Our Founding Fathers understood it to mean that all were equal under the law; all should be equal and free in their pursuit of life, liberty, and happiness. Today, the word has come to mean economic equality; this means that money must be taken from the rich and given to the poor so that everyone is equal in wealth (or lack of it). This is attractive to many people, but we as a nation must again read these perceptive words by Abraham Lincoln:

> We all declare for liberty; but in using the same word we do not all mean the same thing. With some the word liberty may mean for each man to do as he pleases with himself, and the product of his labor; while with others the same word may mean for some men to do as they please with other men, and the product of other men's labor. Here are two, not only different, but incompatible things, called by the same name—liberty. And it follows that each of the things is, by the respective parties called by two different and incompatible names—*liberty* and *tyranny* (italics added).[5]

Unfortunately, given a choice, many people would prefer economic equality along with tyranny rather than economic opportunity with freedom. In free societies, all will not be economically equal. Those who live in a socialistic state become slaves of government regulations and government laws: Citizens become compliant, they accept work quotas and state controlled prices, and because the government seeks to be "fair," the rich are inordinately taxed in order to give benefits to the poor. You obey the master out of whose hand you eat. And, as someone has said, we all desire a life of ease with a high reward. Here is how historian David A. Rausch describes the Hitler era:

> Hitler had lowered wages; state governments and economies were consolidated under the totalitarian regime; and Germany began to rearm. The economy began to recover and men were put back to work but at the high price of personal freedom. Virtually every area of German life was under the control of the Nazi regime, yet most citizens did not seem to care. Fed a steady dosage of propaganda by the press and entertained with massive rallies, parades, and "gifts" from "The Fuhrer," the German people swelled with pride at their nation's apparent comeback.[6]

And so, we, like the German people, are prone to believe the extravagant promises of our politicians because it makes us feel good. Of course, regardless of what we think of Social Security and Medicare, such programs have been of great benefit to many. The challenge is to think clearly about the controversial topic of what government can do and what it should not do. As far as I know, no government in history has had a great record in providing expanded benefits without eventually also expecting more control of its citizens.

There is a fable about a shepherd boy who said to the horse, "You are the noblest beast that treads the earth. You deserve to live in untroubled bliss; and indeed your happiness would be complete were it not for the treacherous stag. But he excels you in fleetness of foot and thus he gets to the water holes before you do. He and his tribe drink up the water far and wide while you and your foal are left to thirst. Stay with me! My wisdom and guidance shall deliver you and your kind from a dismal and ignominious state."

The shepherd boy having tapped into his envy and hatred of the stag, the horse agreed. He yielded to the shepherd lad's bridle; in exchange for more water and a promise of a better life, he lost his freedom and became the shepherd's slave.[7] Today we should be wary of the promise that if we will only accept the bridle, the government will deliver us from our economic woes.

A WORD FROM JESUS

In New Testament times, when Jesus performed the miracle of supplying bread for five thousand people, the masses wanted to make Him a king! Jesus chided them for wanting Him as their king just because He could fill their stomachs. He said, "Do not labor for the food that perishes, but for the food that endures to eternal life, which the Son of Man will give to you" (John 6:27). What He was saying is that physical bread is never as important as spiritual bread. When we come to that fork in the road, we must choose on the basis of principles, not expediency.

Yes, of course, we would all prefer to live even if we had to surrender some of our personal liberties. But as countless Christian martyrs have proved throughout the centuries, there are times when we must draw the line; we must choose to suffer rather than compromise those values that will last forever. Yes, it is better to starve while doing God's will than to be a well-fed Christian who has chosen the short-term advantages instead of divine favor.

We must humbly admit that we do not know what we would do if we were faced with starvation and the deprivation of our families. Perhaps we would fare no better than the Christians in Germany who closed their eyes to atrocities in exchange for the right to live. We can only pray that the economy will never force us to sacrifice the permanent on the altar of the immediate. And when pressed into a corner, let us remember that God is with us. "Keep your life free from love of money, and be content with what you have, for he has said, 'I will never leave you nor forsake you.' So we can confidently say, 'The Lord is my helper; I will not fear; what can man do to me?'" (Hebrews 13:5–6).

The hard road is often the one we must have the courage to choose.

Chapter Three

THAT WHICH IS LEGAL
MIGHT ALSO BE EVIL

HITLER BELIEVED THAT the Jews were subhuman—parasites that needed to be exterminated. In a 1923 speech in Munich, he said, "The Jews are undoubtedly a race, but not human. They cannot be human in the sense of being an image of God, the Eternal. The Jews are the image of the devil. Jewry means the racial tuberculosis of the nations."[1] And, because they were deemed to be in the same category as animals, Hitler made sure they could be killed without reprisals. He would change the law to ensure that extinguishing this race was not a crime.

And thus did Adolf Hitler create new laws that would remove the Jews from their status as persons. With his declaration that they were beneath the animals, Heinrich Himmler had the green light to use his SS troops to exterminate them. The SS was now free to kill without breaking laws; they were free to eliminate Jews without committing murder. There would be no trials for poisoning such vermin;

the land must be cleansed of filth so that it might be peopled with those who have human blood flowing through their veins. If evil is called good, then it becomes good.

Adolf Hitler said so.

THE POWER OF LAWS

Laws reflect a nation's priorities, agenda, and values. In Nazi Germany, where religion was privatized and God was separated from government, not even natural law was recognized as having validity. When Hitler got the Reichstag to give him the power to make the laws, the laws he made were arbitrary, drafted to fulfill the goals of a totalitarian state. The Nazis proclaimed, "Hitler is the law!" As Goering put it, "The law and the will of the Fuehrer are one."[2] Right and wrong was determined by Hitler and his cronies.

The Nuremberg Laws of September 15, 1935, deprived the Jews of German citizenship, confining them to the status of "subjects." These laws forbade either marriage or sexual relationships between Jews and Aryans (Germanic peoples). This was the basis for thirteen administrative regulations against the Jews that would later outlaw them completely. Many of them were deprived of their livelihood and faced starvation. In many towns they were forbidden to purchase food or do business.

Then there were laws against treason. Treason was defined as anything that was contrary to the will and the purposes of the Reich. Criticism was treason; freedom of the press was treason; a failure to further the agenda of the Reich was treason. The Law of Moses was replaced by the law of a man—Hitler.

In 1934, the People's Court was established to try acts of treason. Five judges were appointed to each court, three of whom were always appointed by Hitler or one of his associates "because of their special knowledge in the defense against subversive activities or because they are more intimately connected with the political trends of the nation." The proceedings were secret, the punishments severe. Crimson-red posters announced the names of those who died under the axe of the executioner.

The experience of Nazi Germany reminds us that whoever controls a nation's laws also controls a nation's agenda and its values. R. J. Rushdoony has observed that behind every system of law there is a god: "If the source of law is the individual, then the individual is the god of that system . . . if the source of law is our court then the court is our god. If there is no higher law beyond man, then man is his own god . . . When you choose your authority, you choose your god, and when you look for your law, there is your god."[3] *Look behind the law and there is your god!*

With Hitler's power to make laws, he could mock his powerless opposition. Without a law in their favor, opponents had no defense against the accusations made against them. Pastors, for example, could be tried for "hate crimes" such as "abuse of the pulpit" or "treason" and if accused they had no recourse but to accept their fate. They could easily be presented with false evidence that would accuse them of theft or sexual malpractices. That's why Hitler could belittle the pastors and say with contempt, "You can do anything you want with them. . . . They will submit . . . they are insignificant little people, submissive as dogs, and they sweat with embarrassment when you talk to them."[4] He knew that he could crush their resistance because the law was on his side!

He who creates the laws, wins.

THE BASIS OF LAW

By now it should be clear that the moral landscape of a country is strongly influenced by its laws. When Hitler made the laws, Germany was molded into his own image. As Rushdoony would say, "Show me your laws and I will show you your god."

After Hitler was defeated, war crime trials were held in Nuremberg to judge the guilt of Hitler's henchmen. But a dispute arose as to what laws should be used to try the accused. After all, Hitler's cronies argued, quite plausibly, that they had not broken any laws; their actions were carried out within the protection of their own legal system. They could not be accused of murder because personhood had been redefined to exclude Jews and other undesirables. These men were simply following the laws handed down by the courts of their day. As Eichmann protested before his execution, "I was simply following the laws of war and my flag!" Indeed, Nazism insisted that "it is impossible to measure the laws of the Fuhrer against a higher concept of law because his laws are a direct expression of this *volkisch* [communal life in Germany] concept of law."[5]

Moral relativists who believe that laws are nothing more than the result of social conditioning, subject to the whim of leaders and nations, would have to agree with Goering, Hitler's designated successor, when at Nuremberg he insisted, "This court has no jurisdiction over me, I am a German!" By what laws then, should the Nazis be tried? And what would be the basis of such laws? At Nuremberg, Robert H. Jackson, chief counsel of the United States, argued that there was "a law about the law" that stood in judgment of all men in all countries and societies.[6]

EITHER GOD IS THE
LAWGIVER OR MAN IS.

We must point out in passing that if God does not exist, no such transcendent laws exist. If all laws are relative, and each country has its own idea of what laws they should enact, there is no universal standard by which laws can be judged. Only an appeal to God and revelation can give us the laws by which individuals and countries can be uniformly judged. Even those who would argue that there are certain universal laws based on nature and conscience, they assume (perhaps without knowing it) the existence of God from whom those universal laws are derived. *Without a belief in God, nothing is unconditionally wrong.*

When God is separated from government we are forced to accept arbitrary laws. Either God is the lawgiver or man is; either we derive our laws from theistic universal values, or we say that the individual countries or cultures are the lawgivers. Either God is supreme or the state is supreme.

As you know, in 1973, the United States Supreme Court

changed the law to exclude a whole class of people from constitutional protection. Under the court's ruling and its progeny, the courts have held that as long as a baby was in the womb it was not human and thus could be killed. However, *a court can make abortion legal, but it cannot make it moral.*

Several years ago a group of pro-life protesters who picketed an abortion clinic were sued for slander for calling abortionists murderers. The abortionists argued, just as Hitler's emissaries had done, that they could not be murderers because they were not breaking any laws! The experience of Nuremberg and the silent holocaust in our abortion clinics bear eloquent witness to the fact that when a state is accountable to no one except itself, it simply assumes that whatever is legal is moral. The law is simply whatever the courts or a dictator say it is.

Show me your laws and I will show you your god.

LAW IN EARLY AMERICA

When the Pilgrims came to the United States, they had some definite ideas about God, law, and politics. They came from England where freedom of worship was severely restricted. Reacting against formality and the strictures of the state church, they firmly intended to establish a country based upon principles of freedom. But where could such principles be found? They understood that belief in God was necessary if freedom were to survive. If the state were absolute, it would replace God as the supreme lawgiver. When the Pilgrims signed the Mayflower Compact on November 11, 1620, they pledged themselves in the name of

God and for the glory of God to advance the Christian faith.

The Pilgrims themselves had come from Europe, where wars between the Catholics and Protestants had ended in blood and repression. They came here with the intention of promoting Protestantism, and so objected to other expressions of religious faith. Thanks to Roger Williams and others like him, freedom of religion eventually came to mean that citizens had the genuine freedom to believe or not believe; to accept any religion or none at all.

Later, when the Declaration of Independence and subsequently the Constitution were written, our Founding Fathers emphasized that freedom was rooted in faith in God. A so-called deist, Benjamin Franklin offered what is now a famous acknowledgment of God's sovereignty in the affairs of men:

> I have lived, sir, a long time, and the longer I live, the more convincing proofs I see of this truth—that God governs in the affairs of men. And if a sparrow cannot fall to the ground without His notice, is it probable that an empire can rise without His aid? We have been assured, sir, in the sacred writings, that "except the Lord build the house, they labor in vain that build it." I firmly believe this; and I also believe that without His concurring aid we shall succeed in this political building no better than the builders of Babel.[7]

Today there is a debate as to how Christian the Founding Fathers were, but research has shown that most were Christians, and a few were deists. But whether they were individually Christian or not, there was a general consensus of theism, the belief that God existed. And the new republic was based upon this foundation. This understanding profoundly affected their view of law. Since man was responsible to his Creator, there were absolute standards by which moral judgments could be measured.

A theistic view of law was passed on to the American colonies through Samuel Rutherford's book, *Lex Rex, or The Law and the Prince*, written in 1644. This book was an attack against the divine right of kings and insisted that even princes should be subject to the law.[8] The eighteenth-century jurist William Blackstone also influenced early American understanding of the Bible and nature. Since God is the personal omnipotent Creator, He works and governs the affairs of men. Law should be consistent with His revelation in the Bible and nature (such as the relationship between parents and their children). No law should be passed that would be contrary to the law of God.

This understanding of law emphasized that (1) God is the source of all laws, and (2) all men are created equal. Rutherford had reasoned that since all men are sinners, no man is superior to any other. This meant that even the king had to be subject to the law—there were no exceptions. Notice how these two suppositions were embodied in the Declaration of Independence: "that all Men are created equal, that they are endowed by their Creator with certain unalienable Rights."

These "unalienable" rights were considered absolute rights that stemmed from man's creation by God. He did not have to prove his worthiness; his value was conferred upon him at creation. As a result, man is accountable to an authority higher than other men. All men must recognize that they are under the law of God.

This Christian view of the world so influenced the founding of this nation that in the words of C. Gregg Singer, it "so permeated the Colonial mind that it continued to guide even those who had come to regard the gospel with indifference or hostility. The currents of this orthodoxy were too strong to be easily set aside by those who in their own thinking had come to a different conception of religion and hence of government also."[9]

In years to come, substantial changes would arise in the American understanding of law. With the erosion of a theistic base, law would no longer be based on an absolute view of morality; values would become relative and human worth devalued.

LAW IN TRANSITIONAL AMERICA

The strong influence of Christianity in law in America was weakened by two powerful influences.

First, there was *evolution*. Though Darwin continued to make references to the Creator, he later suggested that man might not have been created at all. Obviously if life had begun by a fortuitous combination of atoms in a distant "warm pond," man would have no obligation toward a deity. But Darwinism was applied to other disciplines as well. Some argued that morals were constantly evolving and that ethics itself was based on "the survival of the fittest." This led to the belief that "might makes right."

Evolutionary theory was also applied to the law. In 1870,

Christopher Langdell, dean of the Harvard School of Law, began to teach that the principles of evolution must be applied to the written opinion of judges. The conclusion was inescapable: Law was not what the *Constitution* said it was but what the *judges* said it was. In other words, there was no longer an objective base; the absolutes dissolved along with the supposed demise of the Creator.[10]

The implications of this new understanding of law were later echoed by Supreme Court Justice Oliver Holmes Jr. when he said that laws are "beliefs that have triumphed and no more."[11] And again he said, "Truth is the majority view of that nation that could lick all the others."[12] And again, "When it comes to a development of a *corpus juris* (or body of law) the ultimate question is what do the dominant forces of the community want and do they want it hard enough to disregard whatever inhibitions may stand in the way."[13] This evolutionary view of law would eventually erode man's dignity and make the arbitrary taking of human life legally possible.

EVOLUTIONARY THOUGHT AND LIBERAL THEOLOGY PROFOUNDLY INFLUENCED THE WAY LAW WAS UNDERSTOOD.

Second, the Christian influence was weakened by the introduction of *liberal theology*. The Bible was stripped of the miraculous and considered as one book among many. No longer was it generally believed that we have in our hands an objective revelation of God. In the end liberalism was reduced to humanism in theological dress.

Evolutionary thought and liberal theology profoundly influenced the way law was understood. No longer was it true that man had certain "unalienable" rights derived from creation. John Warwick Montgomery summarizes how this sad state of affairs came about by pointing out that in the eighteenth century the Bible was killed by unwarranted destructive criticism; in the nineteenth century God was killed; and in the twentieth century inevitably man has been killed. Montgomery adds, "This generation is not accidental; each step logically follows from what has preceded: the loss of the Bible leads to the loss of God, for in the Bible God is most clearly revealed; the loss of God leaves Man at the naked mercy of his fellows, where might makes right."[14]

A student of the history of law in the United States should have been able to predict that human life would soon be reclassified as unworthy of special protection. Abortion, infanticide, euthanasia, homosexual marriage—these are the inevitable results of secular humanism's worldview. When God dies, so does man.

LAW IN MODERN AMERICA

With the fading of the Christian worldview, man now was king and able to make whatever laws he wanted. This has led to what Francis Schaeffer called "sociological law"—the belief that there are no absolutes but rather a relative, evolutionary morality. Law is what the majority wants or what the judges say it is. There is no higher court of appeal; no longer can one challenge a ruling on the basis of absolutes derived from a creator. Man, not God, is the source of laws.

As such, it is no longer possible for some to assert that all men were created equal. Since there was no creation, and we are but an evolving mass of chemicals, it was obvious that man would soon treat his fellows as animals treat their kin. Francis Crick, who won the Nobel Prize for his work in unraveling the DNA code, speaks for many when he says:

> You must realize that much of the political thinking of this country is very difficult to justify biologically. It was valid to say in the period of the American Revolution, when people were oppressed by priests and kings, that all men were created equal. But it doesn't have biological validity. It may have some mystic validity in a religious context, but . . . it's not only biologically not true, it's also biologically undesirable . . . We all know, I think, or are beginning to realize, that the future is in our hands, that we can, to some extent do what we want.[15]

Baby Doe, an infant who starved to death in Indiana because the parents refused to sign a treatment order, was hardly thought of as having been created equal. Because of his handicap, he was considered unfit to live. He was not believed to be endowed by his Creator with certain unalienable rights. Similarly, women who now abort their offspring because they are of the wrong sex do not consider their preborn infants as having the right to "Life, Liberty, and the Pursuit of Happiness." As we weed out weaker animals, so we can now do with mankind.

Although parental consent is needed for the prescribing of most medications, and especially for surgery on a minor, in 1976, a New York court ruled that a girl under the age of eighteen has the right to have an abortion without parental consent. And if the parents do intervene they might, in some instances, be deemed "abusive." Clearly, the Court is intent on encouraging abortion for our nation's young people. And since it creates laws arbitrarily, it can make abortion an absolute right. Unfortunately those who shout that they are "pro-choice!" deny choice to the very person who has the most to lose.

When children's rights are enlarged, parental rights are proportionately diminished.

THE BATTLE FOR THE BENCH

Perhaps now we can better understand why there is so much conflict over the nomination of a person to fill a vacancy on our Supreme Court, or even on the lower courts. Some members of Congress investigate to see whether the nominee gives any hint of having religious convictions; if so they are wary because they know that religious people probably believe in absolutes of some sort and that is not allowable in a day when the Constitution is viewed as a "living document" (subject to the personal whims of the justices).

"It used to be," writes Kay Daly, "that men of God were considered men of principle, that presidents could confidently nominate them, that it was an indicator of integrity, of character, or decency—now it's a one way ticket to a fili-buster."[16] If a nominee is discovered to have had his children homeschooled; if he/she is found to attend church and take his/her faith seriously—for all these reasons the nominee will probably meet tough resistance. Just imagine: *Most of the Founding Fathers would most likely not be approved today because of their religious convictions.*

If the Supreme Court could find that the aborting of pre-born infants is a protected right, though it is not found in the Constitution, then perhaps it will have the flexibility to add other rights, and to restrict past freedoms found in the Con-stitution. After all, the Constitution is a "living document" and like putty can be formed into whatever shape the justices wish. The Constitution is not absolute, the *judges* are.

In the near future, the court might further its humanis-tic agenda by changing some laws and adding others, taking into account our changing culture. We have already seen this in the 2014 Supreme Court decision making same-sex mar-riage the law of the land. Thus we should not be surprised if in the future the Supreme Court or some lower court will reach the following conclusions:

- Laws could be created that would criminalize all public expressions of religion (especially Christianity). This could include severe penalties for those who would pray at any public event, even if the prayer is voluntary and denominationally neutral. All expressions of religion in schools, businesses, government, and the workplace are strictly forbidden. No Bible on a desk, no Christian poster or cross allowed in the workplace.

- All public crosses are to be removed; no memorial in the shape of a cross is permitted.
- Hate crime laws, with their subsequent assertion that "hate speech" is verbal violence, will make any criticism of homosexuals or Muslims punishable, even if the remarks are made in a church or synagogue. This includes readings from the Bible or comments related to the biblical passages. Crimes against homosexuals will be deemed worthy of greater punishment than crimes against others.
- Schools would be legally able to punish any child who does not participate in the celebration of the homosexual lobby and its agenda.
- Reversing a previous decision by the Supreme Court, a new judgment might find that partial-birth abortion is protected by the Constitution. So is euthanasia.
- Parents who oppose their child's decision to have an abortion (even if the child is under eighteen) are held to be abusive and liable to have their children removed from their home. Abortion is thus seen to be an absolute right.
- Churches cannot discriminate against homosexuals in their hiring practices for youth workers, associate pastors, worship leaders, etc. Only the senior pastor can be exempt from this mandate because he is the primary teacher in the congregation.
- Schools can teach homosexuality beginning in the first grade and parents have no right to withdraw the child from these classes.
- Churches that fail to marry homosexuals will lose their tax-exempt status.

- Homeschooling is found to be unconstitutional unless the curriculum is approved by the state school board and the child is tested by the school authorities. He or she must accept contemporary teachings about evolution, sexuality, etc.
- The "Fairness Doctrine" is implemented, which says that whenever a controversial issue is presented (e.g., that Jesus is the only way to God), equal time has to be given to a different point of view in the interest of "fairness." This, in effect, puts an end to Christian radio as we know it.
- Bible studies with more than ten people attending cannot be held in homes without a religious permit that must be furnished by the city/county where the meetings are held.

Pressure to bow to Caesar can be expected to escalate. Secularism will move in slow yet relentless fashion, smashing any opposition that it may encounter. Unless reversed, some form of totalitarianism with its disregard for human freedoms can be expected to emerge. Laws will be deliberately enacted that will cause conflict for those who believe in freedom of religion. And groups like the ACLU know that the average church or ministry cannot bear the legal costs to fight legislation that will shrink personal liberties. The church will be expected to either go along with the changes or face the consequences.

Not surprisingly, when Antichrist arises he will use laws that will indict those who do not worship him. Daniel 7:25 says that he will "change the times and the law." Like Hitler he will begin with lies, then make laws, and finally be worshiped as Lord. His control will be expanded both in numbers and in controlling the details of ordinary living. He will be another Hitler, more powerful, more believable, more blasphemous, more cruel.

Show me your laws and I will show you your god!

TIMES COULD NOT BE BETTER

"Don't you think Jesus is coming soon . . . I don't think things have ever been this bad!" When I hear this from church members, I surprise them by saying, "Seldom have times ever been this good!!!" And I mean it.

Seldom have Christians had it this good!

At the time I am writing this book, we can still broadcast the gospel by radio (even though laws are being discussed that would make this privilege more difficult, if not impossible). We still can witness to our neighbors about Christ, and we can still go to church and gather with other believers without being arrested. This in itself means that we are a privileged people. Through two thousand years of history, the church has seldom had as many freedoms as we do. Throughout the centuries, it has endured reprisals, false accusations, and even death.

We are very grateful for organizations that are dedicated to preserving our freedoms. I thank God for the Alliance Defense Fund (www.alliancedefensefund.org), which has won numerous court battles in preserving the liberties that our Constitution guarantees. Such organizations deserve our respect, prayers, and support. As go the courts, so goes America.

We live at a remarkable time in which God has given us the opportunity to show our faith and courage in a country that in many ways is becoming officially hostile to anything Christian. We should neither be surprised nor think that this is the first time the church has struggled under an oppressive governmental hand.

Let us take a page from the life of three heroes: Shadrach, Meshach, and Abednego. Their king, Nebuchadnezzar, had made a law that they must bow down and worship his image, which he created. But this trio refused and said, "O, Nebuchadnezzar, we do not need to defend ourselves before you in this matter. If we are thrown into the blazing furnace, the God we serve is able to save us from it, and he will rescue us from your hand, O king. *But even if he does not, we want you to know, O King, that we will not serve your gods or worship the image of gold you have set up*" (Daniel 3:17–18b NIV, italics added).

These heroes proved that it is not necessary to have freedom to be faithful. We are not required to win our political battles; we are expected to show our commitment even in the face of threats and sanctions. We must not permit the lawmakers or the courts of America to discourage us from doing what we must: representing Christ in our personal and corporate witness. As our freedoms are curtailed, our witness becomes more focused, more challenging. Let us be obedient to a higher law, the law as given us by the Supreme Court of the Universe.

Him alone we obey; Him alone we worship.
Sola dei Gloria!

Chapter Four

PROPAGANDA CAN
CHANGE A NATION

PROPAGANDA HAS POWER.

Hitler had to learn the hard way that propaganda could serve his purposes even better than a political revolution could. In 1923, he tried to overthrow the Bavarian government by organizing a march through Munich, but it was aborted and ended in failure. He was tried for treason, but given the opportunity to defend himself, and to his delight his speeches were widely read in the newspapers. Already then he knew how to tap into the anger of the German people by railing against the unfair treaty of Versailles and by propagating the widespread belief that the Jews were responsible for the loss of World War I. Hitler knew that the masses could be led if only he could tell convincing lies.

At the end of his trial, he was sentenced to ten months in the Landsberg prison for treason. There he had time to write *Mein Kampf*, in which he outlined a basic plan to implement his agenda. He had time to reflect and to articulate the value of propaganda, and he showed how with a deft use of disinformation, he could almost certainly accomplish what his Brown Shirts could not.

I've taken the time to carefully read what Hitler said about the power of propaganda. He explained the techniques he used to win a hostile crowd to his side. He knew how to tap into their anger, how to handle their objections before they voiced them, and how to get them to see the reasons for his philosophy. In my opinion, he was a master at reading human nature and knowing how to manipulate the masses to gain a zealous following.

THINK OF WHAT HITLER COULD HAVE DONE IF HE COULD HAVE USED TODAY'S MEDIA TO GAIN FOLLOWERS.

Hitler believed that books could never bring about a revolution; only the spoken word, delivered by a person who could connect with his audience could convert them to a radical agenda. He said that when you want to tear down a world and build another in its place you must first of all separate the supporters and the members. The function of propaganda was to attract supporters, and change people's minds so that they would be in agreement with the aims and philosophy of the movement. A member was one who has taken a further step and not only supports the movement but is willing to fight on its behalf. Notice what he wrote in *Mein Kampf*:

> The first task of propaganda is to win people for subsequent organization . . . The second task of propaganda is the disruption of the existing state of affairs and the permeation of this state of affairs with the new doctrine, while the second task of the organization must be the struggle for power, thus to achieve the final success of the doctrine.[1]

Hitler knew that propaganda must be used to prepare the people for something much more drastic, namely, a revolution that would send them down a different path. "The most striking success of a revolution," he wrote, "will always have been achieved when the new philosophy of life as far as possible has been taught to all men, *and if necessary, later forced upon them*."[2] Yes, what begins as information turns out to become the law of the land, and woe to those who dare to oppose the law! "Hate," he said, was "more lasting than dislike." If he portrayed the Germans as victims and the Jews as the victimizers, hatred would fuel his agenda.

It is chilling to think of what Hitler could have done if he could have used today's media to gain followers. His speeches, broadcast on radio and propaganda movies, were persuasive, but with the modern means of instant communication, his task would have been much easier. Thanks to the Internet and television, a passionate leader with an appealing message and the power of oratory could quickly create another cultural movement that would be destructive to the world.

In Hitler's Germany the people were to see and hear only what the government wanted them to see and hear. The Nazis censored film productions and textbooks to be used in schools. Books that did not match the Nazi ideal were burned or outlawed. Children's picture books demeaned the Jews and emphasized the glories of the Aryan race. And it worked.

Of course as any skilled propagandist knows, the masses should never be told the "end-game"; that is, where the leader actually intends to take the people. The masses must not be frightened but reassured that all proposals are for their good. The seamier parts of the agenda should not be revealed and, if they must be, they must be cast in familiar and friendlier terms.

THE POWER OF SLOGANS

In Oceania, George Orwell's chilling totalitarian state in the novel *1984*, we have a compelling description of how the so-called Ministry of Truth used a subtle, sinister language, "Newspeak," to brainwash the people. The slogan of Oceania was "War is peace; freedom is slavery; ignorance is strength." The New Thought Police were able to control the ideas that determined the political and moral views of the culture. The withdrawal of individual freedoms was sold to the population as a plus. *Slavery to the state was presented as the gateway to freedom and prosperity.*

Just so, Hitler knew that terms and slogans could be used for broader appeal. He knew that if he were to accomplish his goals, the capacity for independent thought must be suppressed; thus language must be corrupted to serve sinister ends.

SANITIZED TERMS WERE USED TO CAMOUFLAGE UNSPEAKABLE CRIMES.

Recently I toured Auschwitz, the concentration camp in Poland where 1.2 million people were murdered. When we saw the display of thousands of children's shoes—shoes that belonged to the little ones killed in the camp—we all turned away to find a corner to weep. When Hitler starved children, he called it putting them on a "low-calorie diet." And the extermination of Jews was called "cleansing the land." Euthanasia was referred to as "the best of modern therapy." Children were put to death in "Children's Specialty Centers."

Hitler's cronies seldom said they were going to kill people; even when plans were made to exterminate millions, the leaders spoke only in abstract slogans such as "the final solution." Sanitized terms were used to camouflage unspeakable crimes. Planned massacres were spoken of in clinical terms to mislead the naïve and to assuage the conscience of the perpetrators.

We do the same, of course. No one speaks of killing pre-born infants. Rather, pregnant women are only removing "a product of conception" or a woman is simply "terminating a pregnancy." Politicians speak of being in favor of "a woman's right to choose . . ." but they seldom complete the sentence.

Somehow to say they are in favor of a woman's right to choose to kill her pre-born infant, is too honest, too clear—we might add, and too *chilling*.

Homosexual behavior turns out to be nothing more than "an alternate lifestyle." And adultery is reduced to the more innocuous word: *affair*. Schools that demean religion and promote immorality are said to be "value free," and laws that deny religious speech are promoted as "the fairness doctrine" or simply promoting "localism." Historically, horrendous crimes have been committed in the name of *liberty*.

A WILLING BLINDNESS

I've observed, as I'm sure you have, the power of what I call "a cultural current." That is, a dominant idea promoted by the media and willingly adopted by a critical mass of people who want to believe a myth so badly they will close their minds to all contrary evidence. When such a cultural movement gains momentum, people will stare at facts and filter out what they don't want to believe. Contrary evidence will be ignored or reinterpreted to fit their deepest wishes. And the more people who believe the myth, the more difficult it is for those who wish to counter it. In a spirit of euphoria, all warning signs are brushed aside. *Before we know it, we are in a world where facts do not matter*.

Hitler also believed in cultural movements; he believed that many people would never change their minds individually, but would do so if they were in a crowd of several thousand convinced followers. When a seeker steps into a crowd of thousands, wrote Hitler, that seeker is swept away "into the mighty effect of suggestive intoxication and enthusiasm, when the visible success and agreement of thousands confirm to him the rightness of the new doctrine."[3]

We've all heard the adage, "The nail that stands out is pounded down." Hitler said that doubters are convinced when they find themselves as a minority in the midst of a zealous majority; such an experience causes the doubter to succumb to "the magical influence of what we designate as 'mass suggestion.'"[4] No wonder Hitler said, "How fortunate for governments that the people they administer don't think!"

Perhaps the most enduring lesson of Nazi Germany is that ordinary people, simply concerned about living their own lives, can be motivated to become a part of an evil movement through the power of compelling propaganda, intimidation, and mass euphoria. Yes, it is possible for ordinary people to commit atrocities they never thought possible when they are swept up into a cultural current where everyone is both expected to fall in line and be rewarded for it. In such a climate, anyone who swims against the stream is demonized by misrepresentations, false evidence, and ridicule. With such pressure, even rational and decent people who refuse to be co-opted begin to question their own sanity. Can they alone be right when everyone else is wrong?

Bonhoeffer warned Germany about Hitler when he was declared the chancellor of Germany, but no one listened because they yearned for a strong leader who would lead them into prosperity. So they closed their eyes to Hitler's excesses. Warning signs were overlooked because of this passion of people to believe. And, once the cultural current was widening and flowing with increased speed, anyone swimming upstream was deemed subversive. As Richard Terrell wrote, "Create a critical mass of people who cannot discern meaning and truth from nonsense, and you will have a society ready to fall for the first charismatic leader to come along."[5]

Churchill was right: "The desire to believe something is much more persuasive than rational argument." Like ancient Israel who wanted a king so badly that they refused to listen to God, so people today are prone to want what they want and don't care about the consequences. If everyone wants it, who can resist the momentum? Thus a make-believe world is created where the seamier side of reality is routinely dismissed.

AN AMERICAN MYTH

Think back to the early 1980s when AIDs was repeatedly in the headlines. The homosexual movement in America was devastated, since the virus was most rampant in their communities. The homosexuals knew that the perception that this was a "gay disease" was gaining momentum. The question was, How could these perceptions be changed?

A group of homosexuals decided that they were in need of a propaganda campaign that would change their image. They intentionally used Hitler's methods of propaganda to formulate their approach. In fact, Eric Pollard, the founder of ACT-UP (a militant homosexual group) openly admitted that Hitler's *Mein Kampf* was the model used for the group's strategy.[6] In brief, the strategy is a combination of both lies and intimidation. In referring to Hitler's remark that in matters of propaganda it is always better to tell a big lie than a small one, Eric Pollard quoted from *Mein Kampf*:

The magnitude of a lie always contains a certain factor of credibility, since the great masses of the people in the very bottom of their hearts tend to be corrupted rather than consciously and purposely evil, and that, therefore, in view of the primitive simplicity of their minds, they more easily fall a victim to a big lie than to a little one, since they themselves lie in little things, but would be ashamed of lies that were too big.[7]

He goes on to say that something of a big lie will always remain in people's minds. Then he quotes Hitler, "By clever and persevering use of propaganda even heaven can be represented as hell to the people, and conversely the most wretched life as paradise."[8] Remember, all this is sold under the banner of "tolerance"!

So how do the homosexuals intend to represent heaven as hell and hell as heaven? In 1987, an article was published titled "The Overhauling of Straight America," and in 1990, a book was published titled *After the Ball*, which details their plan. It has succeeded beyond their wildest dreams. And woe to those who swim against this cultural stream!

In their excellent book *The Homosexual Agenda*, authors Sears and Osten outline how the homosexual movement has transformed America. They summarize the methods homosexuals have used to promote their movement and change the attitude of Americans toward their cause. Drawing on their research I will simply give a short overview of the homosexual strategy to illustrate the power of propaganda.

WEAR OUT THE OPPOSITION

The authors of *After the Ball*, Marshall Kirk and Hunter Madsen, say that homosexuals must "talk about gays and gayness as loudly and often as possible." They argue that all behavior begins to look normal if you are exposed to it long enough and at close quarters and among your acquaintances. They write that "the main thing is talk about gayness until the issue becomes thoroughly tiresome."[9] Thus, they want to wear opponents down to the point of total fatigue, until we are willing to give in to their agenda.

In order to do this they say that "in the early stages of the campaign to reach straight America, the masses should not be shocked and repelled by premature exposure to homosexual behavior itself. Instead the imagery of sex should be downplayed and gay rights should be reduced to an abstract social question as much as possible."

The authors knew that they could count on the media to play an important role in their crusade. They added, "The average American watches over seven hours of TV daily. Those hours open up a gateway into the private world of straights, through which a Trojan Horse might be passed."[10] And yes, they have a detailed strategy to infiltrate and demoralize the religious public who might be opposed to their agenda.

APPEAL TO THE EMOTIONS

Hitler, you will recall, said that it was necessary to go beneath rational arguments, and tap into the emotions of an audience. Thus the gay movement's strategy is to "portray gays as victims, not aggressive challengers." They use the language of victimhood, to appeal to Americans' basic sense of fairness and liberal guilt about anyone who claims to have been oppressed. Thus, they have created an atmosphere in which they portray themselves as a victimized class in need of special protections. Of course the buzzwords are *tolerance* and *fairness* and *love*. And portraying themselves as a persecuted minority, they have gained the sympathy of Americans. But as one former homosexual put it, "It's an amazing thing to watch a group that said they were oppressed become the oppressors."[11]

Remember that emotions are more powerful than rational arguments. In short, simply demonize the opposition!

THE CAUSE PORTRAYED AS JUST AND RIGHT

Their third principle is to "give homosexual protectors 'just cause.'" This refers to their strategy of tying their rights to civil rights, saying that they have been wronged just as African-Americans have been in the past. Thus individuals who support their cause are to be motivated by social justice issues, namely, the need to protect homosexual rights from the so-called hostile society. Kirk and Madsen wrote, "A media campaign that casts gays as society's victims and encourages straights to be their protectors must make it easier for those who respond to assert and explain their new perspectives."[12]

Hitler believed that it was necessary to totally destroy the credibility of one's opponents; at no time, he said, should one ever concede that they might be right even on a single point.

The homosexuals agree that they must "make gays look good and make the victimizers look bad." The authors write, "We intend to make the antigays look so nasty that average Americans will want to disassociate themselves from such types."[13]

Never once do the homosexuals concede that one might be against gay marriage because of legitimate religious convictions, natural law, or for the good of families and children. Rather, opponents are called names: bigots, right-wing radicals, persecutors, Nazis, and hate-mongers. Who wants to associate with such people? Again, language is used—powerful imagery is pressed into service—to stifle discussion and rational thought.

Today the media often uses personal attacks against those who dare challenge the homosexual agenda, socialism, or pro-family causes; and regrettably, those on our side of the cultural war sometimes return the favor. Calling people names such as "homophobic" or "hateful" and "religious fanatics" is of course convenient since it spares the critic from having to deal with issues. Hitler was right when he said in effect that one must demonize the opposition if one wishes to create agreement on a political or social philosophy. *Make the price of opposition as steep as possible.*

Lies are used to advance the homosexual agenda. Kirk and Madsen wrote, "It makes no difference that the ads [portraying homosexuals as icons of normality] are lies, not to us . . . not to bigots."[14] The authors say, "Even when it sticks to the facts, propaganda can be unabashedly subjective and one-sided. There is nothing necessarily wrong with this. Propaganda tells its own side of the story as moving (and credibly) as possible, since it can count on its enemies to tell the other side with a vengeance. . . . In its battle for hearts and minds, effective propaganda knows enough to put its best foot forward. This is what our media campaign must do."[15]

The media has joined hands with the homosexual movement in supporting this change of attitude on the part of Americans. The cultural current that we see developing today demonstrates the power of television, newspapers, and the Internet.

Propaganda works.

THE COMPLIANT MEDIA

The media has been a champion of the homosexual agenda. It has promoted gay rights whenever possible, and bowed to the pressure of the gay community. Network comedies are rife with references to adultery, fornication, and homosexuality.

Homosexual characters are always portrayed as loving, kind, and normal, whereas those who are "straight" are generally portrayed as judgmental, angry, and bigoted. Homosexual activists know that humor can be used to desensitize people toward the homosexual lifestyle. Humor is their best weapon to soften up the American public for the promoting of their agenda. If you can get people to laugh at adultery, homosexuality, and even pedophilia, you break down resistance and make the masses more accepting of this behavior.

GLAAD (Gay & Lesbian Alliance Against Defamation) monitors homosexual portrayals in the media. If a homosexual is not portrayed in positive light, GLAAD will pressure the media to bow to the homosexual complaint.

And of course, the media has done a masterful job of shaping the culture's attitudes toward homosexual marriage and the broader gay agenda. Offending homosexuals would be the ultimate sin.

Could you imagine the uproar if Christians were to get an agreement from networks that Christians should never be portrayed in negative light? We'd be branded as hate-filled censors and worse. But the media, acting as a willing arm of the homosexual agenda, is quick to comply with whatever the homosexual watchdog groups want. And those who refuse to be convinced of the rightness of same-sex marriage, for example, are "homophobic" or "hate-mongers."

Alan Sears and Craig Osten write, "On a daily basis, all across America (but more prevalent in some areas of the country than others), children as young as kindergarten are being told that their parents are 'stupid' or 'bigots' or 'intolerant' if they do not accept and embrace homosexual behavior as normal, or even something to be celebrated. In some classes, children are even recruited to promote gay pride marches and events."[16]

The only other group that can, for the most part, depend on positive portrayals in the media is the Muslim community. Networks fear offending Muslims; honor killings sometimes go unreported and the role of women in the Muslim cultures is often overlooked. (Though there have been some noteworthy exceptions.) Despite its history, the Muslim religion is being portrayed as a religion of peace even as evidence to the contrary continues to mount.

Please keep reading.

BETRAYED BY THE ELITES

We can be thankful that the media here in the United States has often played a positive role in being a watchdog in our culture. Government corruption, the plight of the weak or marginalized—these and other worthy causes have often benefited from the light the media sheds on these issues. However, we cannot depend on them to maintain their independence when they are faced with a growing cultural current. In the end they will betray us for ratings, for their own survival, and to avoid offending those groups that have the power to damage or even destroy them.

In Nazi Germany, the elites, who professed a love of freedom, betrayed the people. Hear the words of Albert Einstein, exiled from Germany because he was a Jew:

> Being a lover of freedom, when the [Nazi] revolution came I looked to the universities to defend it, knowing that they had always boasted of their devotion to the cause of truth; but no, the universities took refuge in silence.
>
> Then I looked to the great editors of the newspapers, whose flaming editorials in days gone by had proclaimed their love of freedom; but they, like the universities, were silenced in a few short weeks.
>
> I then addressed myself to the authors, to those who had passed themselves off as the intellectual guides of Germany, and among whom was frequently discussed the question of freedom and its place in modern life. They are, in turn, very dumb.

Only the Church stood squarely across the path of Hitler's campaign for suppressing the truth. I never had any special interest in the Church before, but now I feel a great affection and admiration for it because the Church alone has had the courage and persistence to stand for intellectual truth and moral freedom. I am forced to confess that what I once despised I now praise unreservedly.[17]

We are often critical of the church in the Nazi era, but Einstein knew that the church gave Hitler the only significant opposition he had. The church might not have done all it *should* have done or *could* have done, but it did something! In the final analysis, there were heroes in Germany; there were many who took the risk to withstand the moral bankruptcy of a Nazi regime.

Please note: The universities and the newspapers all ended up swimming along with the Nazi current as it flowed toward the greatest atrocities in history. No matter how much they shouted "Independence!" they simply did not have the courage to oppose a movement that was widely embraced by a culture. They also became a part of the groupthink that made them blind to their bias, blind to their convictions, blind to their calling.

Be assured the same is true (and will be true) in America. Our universities will promote freedom for pornographers, haters of America, and homosexual activists. But don't expect them to extend such freedom to Christian students who reveal their convictions, or speakers who would defend family values or a Christian view of the world. Here in the Chicago area a friend of mine was scheduled to debate with a homosexual activist on a university campus, but just announcing the debate caused such a furor that it had to be postponed. Please note: Even in a debate, an opinion contrary to the homosexual agenda is intolerable! The word *tolerance* doesn't mean what it once did.

With diversity in broadcasting in America, we might think the media will always be forthright in challenging the dominant cultural stream. But wait until all criticism of homosexuality is "hate speech"; wait until laws are enacted that demand that all radio stations have local committees that review what is broadcast; wait until all criticism of Islam is deemed a hate crime; wait until radical Muslims threaten any news outlet that reports "honor killings" in America or expose Sharia law when it is practiced. When there is a high price to be paid for being "fair and balanced," we can be quite sure that all of the news organizations will be silent, even about matters that concern our identity.

Europe is instructive for us. Consider the case of parliamentarian Geert Wilders from the Netherlands. He has spoken out against Islam and has made a movie depicting the plight of women in Muslim cultures. He warns that if Europe does not stop its Islamization, everything will be lost. "We will lose our identity, our culture, our democratic freedoms and our civilization." Predictably bodyguards accompany his every move. (Remember how film director Theo Van Gogh was brutally murdered on the streets of Amsterdam in 2004 for making a provocative movie about the attitudes and treatment of women in the Muslim religion?)

IT IS NOT EASY TO SWIM
AGAINST AN EVER-WIDENING STREAM.

Dr. Wilders says that the elites are betraying Europe. He says the leaders of Europe praise Islam on camera for being a religion of peace but when the cameras are turned off, they are terrified, not knowing how to handle the Muslim threat. They do not have the courage to state their fears and convictions. It is not easy to swim against an ever-widening stream.[18]

And now, as I write, a Dutch appellate court ordered the prosecution of Geert Wilders, charging the filmmaker with "inciting hatred and discrimination" against Muslims for his film exposing the threat of radical Islam. This incident is the latest in a series of attempts by Muslim activist groups and their sympathizers to silence all who would ask hard questions of Islamic theology.

No wonder Muslims join with homosexual activists to support "hate crime" legislation here in America! In 2010, the United Nations considered a resolution that would make all criticism of Islam a crime; unfortunately, Christianity will not be afforded equal treatment. No doubt all this is sold as *tolerance* or as *fairness* or as *equal rights* or as *loving*. No matter what is called, it is still *censorship*.

Canadian pastor Mark Harding, in order to avoid jail time, was sentenced to do 340 hours of community service at the Islamic Society of North America and be indoctrinated under Mohammed Ashraf, the general secretary of the organization. Harding's crime? He opposed his high school's decision to hand out copies of the Quran to students (after the 9/11 terrorist attacks in America) and the school's decision to provide a room for Muslim students to pray. (After all, there were no such concessions for Christians, Jews, etc.) For this he was tried under Canada's "hate crimes" legislation. He received more than three thousand hate-filled calls, many of them death threats. Upon emerging from his trial, he required police protection. So much for freedom of speech in Canada! Yet, the Canadian press, for the most part, ignored the story.[19]

Here in America, an assistant state's attorney told me that until now the church has had a niche where freedom of religion can be exercised. But if and when we have same-sex marriages, churches that refuse to perform such unions will find that their tax-exempt status will soon be revoked. He predicts endless lawsuits that will bankrupt many churches.

We can hear it already, "*All* people have a constitutional right to marriage, in whatever gender arrangement they desire," hence the church is breaking the law by discriminating against those who seek same-sex marriage, or conceivably, by violating a legally protected right to be free of insulting discriminatory action. Then, the next step is to change the law and say that the church has no right to deny homosexuals a marriage ceremony or employment without losing its tax-exempt status.

A few years ago, the Federal Communications Commission proposed that US radio stations set up advisory boards to give input to the stations regarding issues of local interest to provide diversity in programming. The FCC was asked to use its power to renew the licenses of those stations that comply with the new rules, but as yet, we do not know what this will mean in the long term. Does this mean that a Muslim will be on the board of a Christian radio station in an area with a large Muslim population? Or a secularist intent on having airtime for a fair representation for his/her point of view? We will have to wait and see.[20] Thus, despite the First Amendment, a powerful secular government will still seek to control what citizens hear or should not hear.

WHERE DOES THIS LEAVE US?

All of this brings us back to the first century when the believers found themselves living in a pagan regime—with their lives on the line. Rome did not mind if people believed in Jesus; Rome had many gods and if Jesus were just one more among many, that was of no concern to the Roman authorities. What Rome could not tolerate was the idea that Jesus was the *only* way—that He was unique as the Son of God.

If we continue along the path we have chosen as a nation, I have little doubt that preaching the gospel in any context in America will be deemed hate speech. All that will be necessary is for one person to claim they are "offended" by our message and we will have a lawsuit on our hands.

Despite all this, as a church we should be more concerned about glorifying God than we are winning all of these battles. I personally am deeply grateful for those organizations that represent us in Washington and other venues, keeping us up to date on the Congress and raising a voice against legislation that misuses the word *equality* to enact immoral legislation and silence us. And yet, even when we lose, let us show forth the excellency of Christ.

If the present trend continues, we just might have the opportunity to stand with the apostles who were imprisoned and beaten for preaching Jesus—indeed they were warned that they should not speak to anyone about "this name." But they would not be silenced and reported, "Judge for yourselves whether it is right in God's sight to obey you rather than God. For we cannot help speaking about what we have seen and heard" (Acts 4:17–20 NIV).

Hate speech laws will not silence us from preaching the gospel. It is just that in the future some pastors might have to preach it in a different place—in a jail, for instance. Or in a Muslim center.

Propaganda can change a nation, but I pray it will not change us.

Chapter Five

PARENTS—NOT THE STATE—
ARE RESPONSIBLE FOR A CHILD'S TRAINING

IN JANUARY 2008, Germany's youth welfare office and police officials surrounded the Gorber family's Uberlingen home in a surprise raid. Mr. Gorber was visiting his wife at a local hospital where she had been admitted because of pregnancy complications with their ninth child. Despite the children's repeated protests, all but the oldest son, age twenty-one, and the daughter, age twenty, were taken into custody by authorities. Their crime? They refused to send their children to the local public school but instead chose to homeschool their children.[1]

Andre and Frauke R., a Christian family in Hamburg, suffered a similar fate. They chose to educate their children at home on the grounds that they wanted to be obedient to the Lord and keep their children from the influences of the public school system. In response, state officials promised to "apply the full power of the state until this family yielded to compulsory education laws."[2] Their ordeal began with a "coercion" fine of 850 Euros (approximately $1,000). Next, five officers arrested Andre; next, the officers showed up to forcibly escort the children to school. Finally, the family lost custody of the children and they became wards of the state. The family eventually fled to Austria in an RV to join other homeschoolers who have fled Germany so that they could homeschool their children. Although there are some families who are homeschooling in Germany they do so at their own peril, knowing that they too could at any time have a knock on the door and suffer arrest.[3]

Unfortunately, the German media portrays homeschoolers as "extreme fundamentalists," or as belonging to a cult. No matter that children who are homeschooled usually do better than those in the official educational system in all tests. Compulsory public education is mandated not just in Germany but in some other countries of the European Union.

The purpose of this chapter is not to trumpet homeschooling as though it is the only option for concerned parents; there are some public schools in America where learning does take place and the wishes of the parents are honored. And of course there are private schools that might be an alternative. My point, however, lies in a slightly different direction: The fact is that laws making education in public schools compulsory have historically been found in the most totalitarian of governments where state-sponsored indoctrination was a major goal of the educational system. Although it is still legal to homeschool children in America, we can't assume that freedom will continue.

THE SHADOW OF HITLER

Today's law in Germany that makes homeschooling illegal reminds us of a Nazi-era law instigated by Hitler back in 1938. He declared that public education was compulsory and that children could not be educated at home. The state, not the family or church had first dibs regarding the child's education. He understood the value of educating a child:

> The Youth of today is ever the people of tomorrow. For this reason we have set before ourselves the task of inoculating our youth with the spirit of this community of the people at a very early age, at an age when human beings are still unperverted and therefore unspoiled. This Reich stands, and it is building itself up for the future, upon its youth. And this new Reich will give its youth to no one, but will itself take youth and give to youth its own education and its own upbringing.[4]

If Germany was going to be the country Hitler envisioned it to be, the children would have to belong to the Reich. To parents, Hitler calmly said, "Your child belongs to us already . . . what are you? You will pass on. Your descendants, however, now stand in the new camp. In a short time they will know nothing else but this new community."[5]

And in another speech he said, "This new Reich will give its youth to no one, but will itself take youth and give to youth its own education and its own upbringing."[6] Hitler believed quite rightly, that he who controls the youth controls the future. Parents, he insisted, needed to understand the limits of their responsibility; and if they cooperated, all would be well, if not, the law was on Hitler's side! In effect, what Hitler said was that the parents hand the responsibility of raising the child's *body*, but the Reich would educate the child's *soul*.

Private or denominational schools were later closed in Germany due to increased taxes and excessive regulation. Hitler knew that institutions he disliked could be shut down by multiplying laws and by requiring permits for any number of code requirements and procedural regulations. In the end, educational options for parents were squeezed out.

STATE-SPONSORED INDOCTRINATION

The children in Germany were subjected to films that presented the Nazis' view that the Jews were subhuman and that they were an unnecessary burden on society. Darwin's evolutionary notions were also presented in the classroom to extol the virtues of the Aryan race (the Germans) and that the evolutionary idea of survival of the fittest could be hurried along by the extermination of the weak. Since only the fittest survive it makes good sense that "might makes right." Hitler asked, "Why can't we be as cruel as nature?"

With private schools abolished by 1938, all education was unified under the Nazi ideology. Textbooks were rewritten to reflect the view of racial fitness, the rationale for military expansion, and an emphasis on German history and culture. Those who did not fall in line with the Nazi agenda were reprimanded, expelled, or executed. If teachers wanted to keep their jobs, they had to take an oath of loyalty to Hitler.

Even by 1937, 97 percent of the teachers belonged to the National Socialist Teachers' Union. Each teacher had to use the official courses and textbooks prescribed by the Reich. One teacher's manual taught that German children have an inborn aversion to Jews and that intermarriage with Jews is unnatural because it does not follow the natural biological order. Even Jesus was used to promote the Nazi agenda: In some textbooks He was portrayed as a hero who waged war against the Jews until He was betrayed by them and killed.

To my knowledge, the most important source of information regarding Hitler's view of education is found in the book *Nazism: A History in Documents and Eyewitness Accounts*, by Jeremy Noakes and Geoffrey Pridham. They present thirty pages of documents detailing how Nazism attempted to capture the heart of the youth. Hitler could not have been clearer. "German youth must no longer . . . be confronted with the choice of whether they wish to grow up in a spirit of materialism or idealism, of racism or internationalism, of religious or godlessness, but *they must be consciously shaped according to principles which are recognized as correct . . . according to the principles of the ideology of National Socialism*"[7] (italics added).

The purpose of school was not independent thought, but rather to transform the attitude and values of children to conform to what the state wanted. The child, like putty in one's hand, was to be shaped into a true German citizen, meaning, of course, a citizen that surrendered himself/herself to the larger goals of the state.

Hitler's educational philosophy was patterned after that of the Soviet revolutionaries. His goal was to build an army of young radicals who would pay lip service to the past but forge a new path that would ensure that German ideals were passed on from generation to generation. Censorship was practiced. "The teaching . . . aimed to encourage a 'consciousness of being German' . . . In the selection of teaching materials teachers should eschew those works which 'contradict German feelings or paralyze energies necessary for self-assertion' and only those modern works would be selected which 'have an affinity with the spirit of the new Germany.'"[8]

Truth was now defined as that which promoted the Nazi state; the goals of a revived Germany were to take precedence over individual thought and research. For example, "Munich professors [were warned]: 'From now on it is not up to you to decide whether or not something is true, but whether it is in the interest of the National Socialist Revolution.'"[9] Truth was whatever the Nazis preferred it to be.

NOT FACTS, BUT ATTITUDES

Whether history or sociology, Hitler demanded a shift take place in the educational philosophy of the schools; a shift that would no longer be concerned about whether a matter was true or false, but whether it was useful to achieve the ends of the Reich. The values children had derived from their parents needed to be replaced by the new values taught in the classroom. Children had to be indoctrinated and understand that groupthink was more important than the individual. Through psychological pressure, any student who did not agree with the educational agenda stood out as an embarrassment. This, of course, ensured compliance with the unified philosophy of National Socialism, which had freed itself from all absolutes and serious religious considerations.

The educational system became more focused on setting *affective*, not *cognitive* goals (outcomes): "The more enthusiastic they get, the easier are the exams and the sooner they will get a position, a job . . . The new generation has never had much use for education and reading. Now nothing is demanded of them; on the contrary, knowledge is publicly condemned,"[10] wrote Noakes and Pridham. Young people were instructed to encourage their parents to become good Nazis.

In Germany there was an emphasis on teaching right attitudes using the cult of "experience." Unlike knowledge that involves the intellect, experiences that involved feeling provided "access to the deep truths of Nazism which were essentially based on [ideological unity]. Such an 'experience' . . . was regarded as essential to character-building."[11] What the child ate was the parents' responsibility; what he believed and felt was the responsibility of the Reich.

In Germany, as in America today, authority figures would have to be discredited through the experience of what we call "Values Clarification." Many teachers exploited the child's natural desire to be independent from parents and from the church. "It appealed to the desire of youth to be independent of the adult world and exploited the conflict of generations and the typical tendency for young people to challenge authority figures, whether parents or teachers."[12] Parents who tried to contradict what their children were being taught were punished.

Of course, students' values had to be confused before

they could be "clarified." Even in math classes, the ideology of the Reich was promoted. Children were asked questions such as these: "If the construction of a lunatic asylum costs 6 million RM, how many houses at 15,000 RM each could have been built for that amount?"[13] The goal, of course, was to get students to shed their natural inclination to sympathize with the needs of lunatics (read anyone who didn't agree with the Reich) and to see such issues through pragmatic, economic eyes.

Hitler understood that young people are very conscious of what their peers believe—how they dress and talk. "The slogan 'youth must be led by youth' . . . was ritually echoed and to some extent followed in practice. But the spirit in which it was applied was very different. These young leaders were not representing an autonomous youth culture but were functionaries of an official bureaucracy regimented by rules and regulations and following set patterns of training."[14] Even as they were being indoctrinated, young people were given the "freedom" to form their own clubs and peer groups, just as long as they promoted rebellion against parents and church, and as long as they advanced the larger, grander cause of National Socialism. Group peer pressure was used to silence, if not change the mind of any student who still believed in the values of home and church.

Teachers were expected to develop an optimistic atmosphere of victory, of confidence, and of the certainty of Germany's success. "All other values were subsumed under this rubric. Through arts, crafts, and multicultural experiences the children were indoctrinated."[15] The point, of course, was to condition students to compliance. "It was preferred that people should not have a will of their own and should totally subordinate themselves,"[16] write Pridham and Noakes.

All of us know there is no such thing as a completely unbiased historian. Even choosing a curriculum—deciding what should be included and what should be left out—in all such decisions human bias is brought into the educational process. What makes Nazi Germany unique is the way in which facts were deliberately distorted to promote an agenda. Lies were taught: lies about Jews, lies about Germany's history, and lies about Hitler's intentions.

Hitler knew, as all of us do, that feelings can be more powerful than reason. And, unless feelings are changed, the mind will revert to its former patterns of thought. Centuries ago in the garden of Eden, Satan in effect said to Eve, *"Feel, don't think!"* Thinking can change feelings; but *feelings can also change thinking.* The point, of course is that a person should not pay attention to facts, but give credence to how he or she feels.

There was a great deal of emphasis on the relevance of courses to Germany's present historical and sociological situation. "The course of history must not appear to our young people as a chronicle which strings events together indiscriminately, but, as in a play, only the important events, those which have a major impact on life, should be portrayed."[17] Thus a false world was created by carefully selecting the curriculum and eliminating anything that did not promote the politically correct ideology.

This philosophy was carried over into all disciplines. The only criterion for the curriculum was whether the students understood the Reich's worldview. "New courses were introduced in such fields as racial studies, eugenics, and defense studies and there was a new emphasis on pre-history ... Law and political science courses were adapted to fit in with the changes introduced by the regime."[18]

Education was life-related, experience-centered, and adopted with group pressure. You either conformed as a teacher or student or faced the consequences.

AMERICAN VALUES CLARIFIED

Unfortunately, our schools are all too often indoctrination chambers where children come to be scrubbed of their trust of parents, their church, and their sexual identity, and are force-fed a diet of secularism and immorality. Many years ago Dr. Chester Pierce of Harvard University, addressing two thousand teachers in Denver, made a chilling assessment of the teachers' responsibility. Of course his extreme comments are not shared by all teachers—indeed there are some public schools that are still committed to education and not indoctrination—but it is indicative of a trend in our schools that cannot be ignored.

> Every child in America who enters school at the age of five is mentally ill, because he comes to school with allegiance toward our elected officials, toward our founding fathers, toward our institutions, toward the preservation of this form of government ... Patriotism, nationalism, sovereignty, all that proves that children are sick because the truly well individual is one who has rejected all of those things and is what I would call the true international child of the future.[19]

How are these changes brought about?

Values clarification was invented by Dr. Sidney Simon in order to change the beliefs, convictions, and moral values of a child. It is based on the notion that there are no absolutes—no right or wrong. Such transformation is to come into the life of a child by affirming the following: (1) personal values should be left up to each student, not dictated by parents or the church, and (2) questions are to be used that solicit open-ended answers to teach the child that there are no absolutes. Examples of such questions include: Would you favor a law that would limit the size of families to two children? Do you think parents should teach their children to masturbate? Do you think sex education should include techniques for love-making and contraception? Would you like to have different parents? How often do you have sex?[20]

THE CHILD'S VALUES ARE AS GOOD AS ANYONE ELSE'S AND NO ONE CAN TELL HIM ANY DIFFERENT.

Now that the child has been stripped of his previous values, three more steps follow: (3) the teacher is to tell the child that he must make up his own mind as to what values he will accept (at this point the child is subject to psychological manipulation), and then (4) the child must publicly declare his "conversion" to the new values systems. He is told he must stand before his peers and tell them what his new values are. Then (5) the child is to regularly act on these values. In the end, the child firmly believes that no one—neither his parents or his church or the Bible—has the right to tell him what is right and what is wrong. Because all values are preferences, they are not subject to argument or to be judged by any other authority. The child's values are as good as anyone else's and no one can tell him any different.[21]

The students are then force-fed the idea that if they still have conflicts in their mind, they must realize it is possible to hold two points of view, no matter how contradictory they may appear. With this accomplished, the child is now defenseless against an onslaught of humanistic beliefs: evolution; socialism; the normalcy of homosexuality, abortion, euthanasia, etc. Then the student is told that consensus on these issues is reached through group discussion. The child does not know that the values that will be adopted by the group are predetermined by the curriculum. This is a field-tested methodology that has been used successfully in communist countries; now it operates in many of our nation's classrooms.[22]

THE SEXUALIZATION OF CHILDREN

On May 22, 2009, a headline read, "Gay Curriculum Riles Elementary School Parents." It reports that parents say they are being bullied by school administrators into accepting a new curriculum that includes compulsory lessons about the lesbian, gay, bisexual, and transgender community that will be taught to children as young as five years old.

These parents, in the district of Alameda, a suburb of

San Francisco, also say that they will not be allowed to keep their children out of such classes. Attorneys for the school board agree that, if the curriculum is adopted, the parents will have no legal right to remove their children from the classes. Obviously, the First Amendment rights of parents are ignored; and even though most parents oppose the plan— their opinions have no effect.[23]

Why this desire to sexualize children? Tammy Bruce, who is a past president of the Los Angeles Chapter of The National Organization for Women, was a firsthand witness of attempts by "progressive" political groups to undermine our millennia- old code of morals and values. Now she exposes the liberal social agenda and says that these groups have the intention of reordering society as we know it. They are intent on *bending society to mirror their warped view of the world.*

Since this is a chapter on the education of children, I shall quote one of her passages at length. It deserves a careful read:

> Today's gay activists have carried the campaign a step fur-
> ther, invading children's lives by wrapping themselves in the
> banner of tolerance. It is literally the equivalent of the wolf
> coming to your door dressed as your grandmother.
>
> The radicals in control of the gay establishment want
> children in their world of moral decay, lack of self-restraint,
> and moral relativism. Why? How better to truly belong to
> the majority (when you're really on the fringe) than by
> taking possession of the next generation? By targeting chil-
> dren, you can start indoctrinating the next generation with
> the false construct that gay people deserve special treatment
> and special laws. How else can the gay establishment actually

get society to believe, borrowing from George Orwell, that gay people are indeed more equal than others? Of course, the only way to get that idea accepted is to condition people into nihilism that forbids morality and judgment.[24]

Tammy Bruce believes the reason these ideas are widely accepted is that "sexualizing children" as she calls it, guarantees control of the culture for future generations. She writes, "It also promises sex-addicted future consumers on which the porn industry relies. By destroying those lives, they strike the final blow to family, faith, tradition, decency, and judgment."[25]

Yes, it is to the advantage of the radical left to have a sex-addicted culture! Parents often have no idea that these techniques are being used on their children. They do not know that sex education classes are often little more than "how to" classes—how to have sex without guilt and without a baby. They do not realize that teachers in North Carolina, for example, were told what values they should instill in their children. The seven-point list:

- There is no right or wrong, only conditioned responses.
- The collective good is more important than the individual.
- Consensus is more important than principle.
- Flexibility is more important than accomplishment.
- Nothing is permanent, except change.
- All ethics are situational; there are no moral absolutes.
- There are no perpetrators, only victims.[26]

Again, I must emphasize that all public schools do not subscribe to these agendas, but parents must investigate what their children are being taught. If not, our children are mentally confiscated by an intentional humanistic point of view.

POLITICALLY CORRECT TEXTBOOKS

As I was writing this book, I watched a special on television dedicated to the $10 billion–dollar textbook industry here in America. I was not surprised but deeply grieved at what I learned. Some of the textbooks in American history do not mention the Pilgrims in order that all groups might have "equal opportunity." America is presented in a negative light as an oppressive, capitalistic country, without an equally critical assessment of other countries and cultures. One history textbook mentions the terrorist attacks of 9/11, but nowhere does it indicate that the terrorists were Muslims. Thanks to Muslim committee members, Islam was presented as a historical fact but Christianity and Judaism were couched in the language of doubt along these lines, "It is said that Moses received the ten commandments; and it was believed that Jesus was the Messiah," etc.

And yes, I should mention that the language police were at work—yes, they do exist! The TV special reported that the word *snowman* is replaced by *snow person*, in one textbook. No pictures were allowed of a woman in the kitchen for that too is a kind of stereotype that must be avoided.[27]

In college your child can expect that history just might be taught as a weapon to be used to promote certain agendas. Many in the politically correct (PC) movement believe that the purpose of history is to redress past wrongs. American history is deemed as racist, sexist, and classist and therefore must be considered primarily as the history of oppression. The crimes of Europeans are emphasized. The positive contributions of European society (some think there are none) must be swept aside.

When the University of Pennsylvania announced mandatory "racism seminars" for students, one student expressed her concerns by saying that she had a "'deep regard for the individual and my desire to protect the freedoms of *all* members of society.' A university administrator sent her note back with the word 'individual' circled and the comment, 'This is a RED FLAG phrase today, which is considered by many to be RACIST. Arguments that champion the individual over the group ultimately privilege "individuals" who belong to the largest or dominant group".'"[28]

"In PC land, the middle ground disappears," educator Les Parrott explains. "Either you are pro-gay rights or you are homophobic. Either you are fighting for feminist causes or you are a chauvinist."[29] In the PC world no one can be opposed to abortion on the grounds that it is the killing of human beings. One can only be opposed because one is sexist, opposed to women's rights, and on the side of oppression. Homosexuality cannot be opposed on the grounds that it is condemned in the Bible or violates natural law. Those who oppose it do so because they are homophobic, morally oppressive, and hate-mongers. God cannot be called Father because one adheres to the Bible; those who refer to God as male are sexist.

The most important assumption of the PC movement is

that there is no objective truth—either in history or morality. Truth is changing, and the truth of the moment arises out of the particular social/ethnic context. Like the Marxists, PC advocates see history as primarily a record of class struggle and oppression. The basic axiom is that the poor are poor because the rich are rich. The rich are oppressors and the poor are the victims. The capitalism of wealthy nations is the cause of all the poverty in other countries.

Now we can better understand why the PC movement believes that history can be rewritten to accommodate the wishes of oppressed minorities. History cannot be considered in any sense an objective study of the past along with a sincere attempt to interpret its causes and effects; rather, history is a weapon to be used for whatever purposes seem appropriate for those who are oppressed. It can be molded into whatever shape best suits the liberal agenda.

WHAT ARE YOUR CHILDREN BEING TAUGHT?

Here is a random list of what is happening in some of our schools:

* Some schools use textbooks that favor Islam and that denigrate Christianity.[30]
* In some colleges administrators or professors would not allow students to give pro-American speeches on campus after the 9/11 attacks of 2001, telling the students that America was the aggressor.[31] On these campuses the American flag was spoken of as "divisive" and not to be honored.

- Marxist ideology often dominates college classrooms. David Horowitz said, "There are more Marxists on the faculties of American colleges than in the entire former communist bloc."[32]
- A California teacher has been forbidden to show his students the Declaration of Independence because it refers to God. In fact, according to one judge, the Constitution itself was deemed unconstitutional.[33]
- In many schools the family is redefined as a "unit of two or more persons, related either by birth or by choice, who may or may not live together, who try to meet each other's needs and share common goals and interests . . ."

A FINAL PLEA

As I close this chapter, I can only plead with you as a parent to take charge of your child's education. For some, this will mean homeschooling; for others a private school; and for those in the public school, it will mean working closely with teachers, school boards, and administrators to monitor what is happening in your child's life. There are no easy answers, but our children are our most precious possession.

If you want to investigate homeschooling, there are several organizations dedicated to helping you understand its benefits and giving you the direction you need. The Home School Legal Defense Association (www.hslda.org) works to preserve the freedoms necessary for those who intend to have their children taught at home, and keeps you up to date on the latest homeschooling news. The Exodus Mandate (www.exodusmandate.org/) is designed to help you understand the hows and whys of homeschooling and will also inform you on what is happening in our schools. Both of these organizations give you the resources you need to make a wise and calculated decision if you are contemplating having your children taught at home.

God places the responsibility for the children's training on the parents, particularly the father and the passing of the faith to subsequent generations. "And these words that I command you today shall be on your heart. You shall teach them diligently to your children, and shall talk of them when you sit in your house, and when you walk by the way, and when you lie down, and when you rise" (Deuteronomy 6:6–7).

God has not only entrusted the body of your child to your care, but also his/her soul. We cannot let our public educators take over the hearts of those who are most vulnerable and precious to us. If ever parents must be courageous, it is now.

Chapter Six

ORDINARY HEROES
CAN MAKE A DIFFERENCE

WHEN GOD CALLS a man, he bids him come and die," wrote Dietrich Bonhoeffer during the dark days when the church in Germany was being Nazified. And at the age of thirty-nine, he practiced what he preached; he was hanged on the gallows and died.

He wrote:

> Cheap grace is the deadly enemy of our Church. We are fighting today for costly grace. Cheap grace means grace sold on the market like cheapjacks' wares. The sacraments, the forgiveness of sin, and the consolations of religion are thrown away at cut prices.... In such a Church the world finds a cheap covering for its sins; no contrition is required, still less any real desire to be delivered from sin.... Cheap grace means the justification of sin without the justification of the sinner.... Cheap grace is grace without discipleship,

grace without the cross, grace without Jesus Christ, living and incarnate.[1]

With these words and a life to back them up, Dietrich Bonhoeffer became a powerful spokesman for a form of vibrant Christianity that was independent of state interference. This man who called the church back to its mission would eventually become a martyr for his part in a conspiracy to assassinate Hitler. At great personal cost he raised a flag, but few paused to salute—but those who did, deserve to be honored even as he was.

Bonhoeffer was not just an ordinary hero but an extraordinary one, both in his stature as a Christian leader, and as a Christian intellectual. But thousands of lesser-known people were inspired by his example and became a credit to the Christ they served. Thanks to his courageous witness, hundreds of pastors ended up in concentration camps willing to suffer and die for their faith. If every pastor would have been a Bonhoeffer or a Niemoller, Hitler could not have accomplished his agenda. The pastors and their congregations would have simply said, "No" to the Nazi doctrine of the superiority of the Aryan race and its frightful implications.

Today in America we need an army of ordinary heroes to stand against the gathering darkness in our land. We need people who will stand for truth courageously, consistently, and with humility and grace. We need millions of believers who will represent Christ in the various vocations of America. We need to enlist people who know what they believe, why they believe it, and how to live out their convictions in diverse situations. We need those who are willing to pay the price of discipleship and obedience and to do so with joy.

A tall order, but possible.

INSPIRED BY COSTLY GRACE

Of course I am not saying that we in America are being called upon to suffer in the same way as the Christians in Germany did. Someday that might be our lot, but as of now we are simply confronted with a growing hostility toward the Christian faith both in the popular culture and in our legal system that seems intent on creating laws that limit our freedoms. We need to individually draw a line in the sand, making up our minds that we will not compromise our principles, even at great personal cost.

Those of us who live in America think that suffering for Christ is somehow fundamentally inadmissible; it is un-American and contradicts the notion that I should do "what is best for me." As a result of our aversion to this badge of honor, Christian students in our universities, fearing the consequences of disagreeing with "politically correct" agendas, often fall silent about their faith in Christ to avoid stirring the academic waters so that they will be permitted to graduate.

An InterVarsity Christian Fellowship campus minister told a reporter for *Christianity Today* that "Christians are not singled out unless they believe there is a hell or talk about abortion." The reason, he says, that attacks against Christians at the university seldom get personal is that very few students are willing to jeopardize their status by defending their views. Already years ago, Nathan Chan, a Christian enrolled at Stanford Graduate School, said, "If you take [multiculturalism] to an extreme it is very individualistic, you have your own bias, and you can think what you want in that box, so long as you don't affect others' boxes. When you say that Christianity is the only truth, you are imposing on someone's box."[2]

But if Christians are silent at our universities for fear of being disgraced; if believers are intimidated at work because of new laws that might keep religion out of the workplace; if a Christian nurse is silent about abortion because to speak out would put her job in jeopardy; in short, if we keep Christ to ourselves out of fear of reprisals, are we not taking our stand with those pastors in Germany who chose to close ranks with Hitler? Is not our sin even greater since the consequences of our obedience to Christ is so minimal in comparison with what they faced? Are we qualified to sit in judgment of the church in Germany if we ourselves have never lost a job or failed a course because we are Christians?

I believe that the spiritual climate of America will never be changed unless we have a revival of what we used to call "the layman." That is, we need ordinary people living authentically for Christ in their vocations, among their neighbors, and in positions of influence. We cannot look to a man or even a movement as much as to the common person who is committed to Christ and living for Him.

Sometimes the gospel has to be communicated with more than words. Michael Baumgarten, a nineteenth-century Lutheran pastor who was excommunicated from his church, wrote, "There are times in which lectures and publications no longer suffice to communicate the necessary truth. At such times the deeds and sufferings of the saints must create a new alphabet in order to reveal again the secret of truth."[3] Suffering communicates the gospel in a new language; it authenticates the syllables that flow so easily from our lips. When the chaff is separated from the wheat, the kernels germinate and grow. *It is not how loud we can shout but how well we can suffer that will convince the world of the integrity of our message.*

Bonhoeffer said accurately, "Suffering is not an interruption, but our calling." Paul wrote that we are to share in the sufferings of Christ. This is the pain we endure because of Christ; the choices we make because He is our example. In our suffering we conform to the likeness of Christ. Let me repeat: He *calls* us to suffer.

As our culture drifts into paganism, we as Christians fear the suffering that might come our way. Employees fear that they might not be able to witness for Christ given new laws that declare that workplaces are "religion free." Parents are increasingly isolated from the school systems that promote homosexual lifestyles, sexual freedom, and radical individualism. A day could come when churches would fear losing their tax-exempt status if they refused to marry homosexual couples.

Such suffering, indeed, *any* suffering for Christ in our culture is largely unknown to us. But other countries have not been exempt; in fact, there are more people dying for their faith in the face of hostile cultures and political regimes than at any time in history. Perhaps our time will come.

PEOPLE WHO HAVE MADE A DIFFERENCE

The list of Christian heroes, both past and present, is long and impressive. I've just chosen a few who have inspired me to stand for the truth of the gospel because of their un-wavering commitment to God rather than themselves. We might regard them as being "extraordinary" because of their prominence, but they are ordinary men and women, whose courage has thrust them into positions of influence.

Zakaria Botros

A recent hero of mine is a Coptic priest named Zakaria Botros, a man who through his television program and the Internet preaches the gospel to fifty million Muslims in the Middle East each week. Best of all, tens of thousands of Muslims have come to saving faith in Christ through his ministry.

I became acquainted with this man's ministry when *World* magazine nominated him as "Daniel of the Year" in 2008. He spoke at The Moody Church under heavy security since jihadist groups have reportedly posted a death threat of $50 million on his head. He is regarded as Islam's public enemy number one.

After his talk in which he exposed the deceptions of Islam, I asked him this question, "What price have you had to pay for your boldness in pointing out the errors of Islam and sharing the claims of the gospel?"

His answer surprised me for its simplicity and authenticity. He said, "Whatever price I have had to pay is cheap in comparison to what Jesus Christ has done for me in shedding His blood for us!" Then he explained how his brother had his tongue cut out and a stake put through his head for preaching the gospel in Egypt. But that was okay if it was the price that needed to be paid for preaching the gospel.

Where does this man get his courage, living as he does

with constant death threats and the knowledge that he is Islam's number one public enemy? "Jesus takes care of me until it is my time to go."

What it comes down to is a question: Is what we as Christians believe the truth? Or is it not? If yes, then we should not be intimidated by our culture.

Many Muslims who have converted to Christ say that they are willing to come out of hiding, so to speak, because of Dr. Botros's bold witness. How refreshing to find a man who is so bold and yet loving in his witness, that not even Islam can silence him!

May God give us millions of such "ordinary" heroes!

Corrie ten Boom

Corrie was living with her family when Holland surrendered to the Nazis. She was forty-eight, unmarried, and worked as a watchmaker in the shop that her grandfather had started in 1837. Corrie credits her father's example in inspiring her to help the Jews of Holland. She tells of an incident in which she asked a pastor who was visiting their home to help shield a mother and newborn infant. He replied, "No, definitely not. We could lose our lives for that Jewish child!" She went on to say, "Unseen by either of us, Father had appeared in the doorway. 'Give the child to me, Corrie,' he said. Father held the baby close, his white beard brushed its cheek, looking into the little face with eyes as blue and innocent as the baby's own.... 'You say we could lose our lives for this child. I would consider that the greatest honor that could come to my family.'"[4]

She and her family were arrested in 1944. Her father

died a few days later but Corrie and her older sister, Betsie, remained in a series of prisons and concentration camps, first in Holland, and later in Germany. They used their horrendous circumstances to share the gospel and give comfort to other inmates. Her sister died in a concentration camp, but through a clerical error, Corrie was released.

Her story of how she forgave her captors who had so brutally abused and humiliated her and her sister, has captured the minds of millions. One line from her book *The Hiding Place* I will never forget is, "There is no pit so deep that God's love is not deeper still."

Corrie died in 1983, an authentic hero, reminding us that some things are more important than life itself. And, we must forgive others, even as we have been forgiven.

Charles Colson

More than forty years ago, Charles W. Colson was not thinking about reaching out to prison inmates or reforming the US penal system. In fact, this aide to President Richard Nixon was "incapable of humanitarian thought," according to the media of the mid-1970s. Colson was known as the White House "hatchet man," a man feared by even the most powerful politicos during his four years of service to President Nixon.

When news of Colson's conversion to Christianity leaked to the press in 1973, the *Boston Globe* reported, "If Mr. Colson can repent of his sins, there just has to be hope for everybody." Colson would agree. He admits he was guilty of political "dirty tricks" and willing to do almost anything for the cause of his president and his party.

After serving seven months in prison, he left with a vision to do something to help the men he had met behind bars. So he began Prison Fellowship, and today thousands upon thousands of Christian voluntees and churches in 113 countries around the world visit prisons to mentor prisoners, help their families, and to share the good news of Christ with them.

Of course, Colson received opposition from the ACLU and other groups who oppose sharing the gospel message. But despite opposition, Prison Fellowship continues to share the gospel and live with the consequences.

Colson proved that the gospel can save notorious sinners and then use them to share the good news with others. No one is beyond hope; no one has fallen so far, but that God's grace can reach them.

Donnita Travis

Donnita Travis is probably not a name familiar to all who read this book, but she is a genuine hero, a woman who is making a difference in a world where others have long since concluded that no difference can be made. Thanks to her vision and leadership, the lives of children and families are being changed in the inner-city neighborhoods of Chicago. The hope of the gospel is penetrating the most drug-infested, crime-ridden neighborhoods where 85 percent of the children are growing up without a father in the home. The gospel is being implanted in these neighborhoods thanks to the vision, tenacity, and faith of one woman.

Several years ago Donnita, a member of The Moody Church, went on a personal retreat to ask God a question: What do You want me to do with the rest of my life? God laid children on her heart, so she signed up to help the church with its children's ministry. Soon she was beginning a ministry that would become known as "By the Hand Club for Kids," an after-school program with a radical agenda: teaching children how to read, how to hone their skills, and how to become followers of Christ.

By the Hand Club for Kids is not just another after-school program. The teachers are full-time employees who devote themselves to the holistic needs of the children—mind, body, and soul. Only children most in need of critical intervention are allowed into the program, and the results have been so astounding that the program has caught the attention of Chicago's mayor and the city's school board. With a budget of $5 million, which has to be raised annually, Donnita has shown through her faith and leadership that shining a light in a dark place is much more effective than cursing the darkness.

Ordinary heroes can do extraordinary things for God.

Unsung Heroes

Of course there are tens of thousands of heroes whose names are unknown, but who serve the Lord with courage and distinction. Here in America we have honest attorneys who are more interested in justice than in winning; there are teenagers who witness in their schools despite threats from the ACLU; there are doctors who refuse to cooperate with deceptive colleagues; and, thanks be to God, we have politicians who would rather lose an election than compromise their values.

Only through such an army of committed followers of

Christ can we hope to stem the relentless flow of secularism, eroticism, and the damning influence of "intolerance" that would close the mouths of Christian believers.

QUALITIES OF CHARACTER

What makes a strong Christian? What are the characteristics of those who are willing to let their convictions be known as a student in a university knowing it could jeopardize their standing? What drives those who serve with integrity in a corporation even though they know that their colleagues resent it? And, more importantly, what makes church leaders continue to preach the "whole counsel of God" despite threats of a lawsuit?

A man who studied the character of those who are willing to withstand opposition and even persecution tells us that courageous believers are those who (1) know the power of prayer and fasting, (2) can recite large portions of Scripture and hymns, (3) count it an honor to suffer for Christ's sake, and (4) know that suffering is normal, it is one of the gifts God gives to the church.[5]

I have no doubt that these qualities of character are needed to authenticate our message. So we must ask: Are these the kind of Christians we are producing in our churches, Bible colleges, and seminaries? And are we teaching our people how to represent Christ in a hostile environment? After all, it is our lives that must back up our words.

In his book *A Severe Mercy*, Sheldon Vanauken describes his first encounter with Christians. You have to read the words he wrote that night in his diary.

The best argument for Christianity is Christians: their joy, their certainty, their completeness. But the strongest argument *against* Christianity is also Christians—when they are sombre and joyless, when they are self-righteous and smug in complacent consecration, when they are narrow and repressive, then Christianity dies a thousand deaths. . . . Indeed there are impressive indications that the positive quality of joy is in Christianity—and possibly nowhere else. If that were certain, it would be proof of a very high order.[6]

Our joylessness counts negatively when it comes to sharing our Christian witness. We need to remember that we are to respond in unexpected ways to the trials that come our way. Not with pride or judgmentalism; not with harsh words or complaining, but representatives of Christ. To quote Bonhoeffer once more, "Where the world exploits, [the Christian] will dispossess himself, and where the world oppresses, he will stoop down and raise up the oppressed. If the world refuses justice, the Christian will pursue mercy, and if the world takes refuge in lies, he will open his mouth for the dumb, and bear testimony to the truth . . . for Jew or Greek, bond or free, strong or weak, noble or base."[7]

The church was birthed in the crucible of suffering and opposition. Paul wrote about his own experience, "To the present hour we hunger and thirst, we are poorly dressed and buffeted and homeless, and we labor, working with our own hands. When reviled, we bless; when persecuted, we endure; when slandered, we entreat. We have become, and are still, like the scum of the world, the refuse of all things" (1 Corinthians 4:11–13). Now, as Americans we can no longer take for granted that we live in a country where we can expect the government and the courts to be favorable to us. But we accept this as our calling; we simply choose to stand for truth with love and grace.

WINNING WHILE WE LOSE

It is not necessary for us to win our battles in order to be faithful to our calling. Many people in past history have not won in this life, but there is no doubt they were winners in the life to come. Just think of the martyrs who knew that losing often is winning. As Jesus put it, "To lose your life is to find it; to find it is to lose it."

Even if we are faithful we might not "win" in our ideological battle with a hostile culture bent on using the courts to scrub the public square clean of any reference to God. But we are neither discouraged nor daunted, for we know that God rules and in the end He will demonstrate His power and righteousness.

Peter Marshall was right, "It is better to fail in a cause that will ultimately succeed, than to succeed in a cause that will ultimately fail." Better to fail while serving God than to win while serving oneself. Better to die sharing the gospel than to live denying the Christ who purchased us. Let us not let compromise eclipse courage.

God's word to us is clear:

Do all things without grumbling or questioning, that you
may be blameless and innocent, children of God without
blemish in the midst of a crooked and twisted generation,

among whom you shine as lights in the world, holding fast to the word of life, so that in the day of Christ I may be proud that I did not run in vain or labor in vain. (Philippians 2:14–16)

Let's pray that God will give us people who shine as lights in a dark world; they are ordinary heroes but they are extraordinary to God! And they make a difference!

Chapter Seven

WE MUST EXALT THE CROSS
IN THE GATHERING DARKNESS

CONFESS! CONFESS! CONFESS!"

Yes, as you might have guessed, Bonhoeffer was speaking. He was attempting to awaken the church to its responsibility at an hour when its witness and strength was most sorely needed. He insisted that if the church stood upon Christ as the rock, "the church will not be taken from us—its name is decision, its name is discerning of the spirits. . . . Come you who have been left alone, you who have lost the church, let us return to Holy Writ, let us go forth and seek the church together. . . . For the times, which are times of collapse to the human understanding may well be for her a great time of building . . . Church, remain a church, . . . Confess! Confess! Confess!" he pleaded.[1]

The date was July 23, 1933. In January of the same year, Hitler had been installed as chancellor of Germany. The very next day, this young man who was not duped by der Fuhrer's intentions, gave a radio address in which he warned that when a people idolize a leader, "then the image of the leader will gradually become the image of the 'misleader.' Thus the leader makes an idol of himself and mocks God." Before these last sentences were broadcast, Bonhoeffer's microphone had been mysteriously switched off.

Bonhoeffer kept reminding anyone who would listen that the church has only one altar before which it must kneel and that is the altar of the Almighty. He contrasted the proud Nazi agenda with the humiliation of Christ on the cross. "God's victory means our defeat, it means our humiliation; it means God's mocking anger at all human arrogance, being puffed up, trying to be important in our own right. It means the Cross above the world . . . The cross of Christ, that means the bitter scorn of God for all human heights, bitter suffering of God in all human depths, the rule of God over the whole world . . . with Gideon we kneel before the altar and say, 'Lord on the Cross, be thou alone our Lord. Amen.'"[2]

Bonhoeffer warned that if the church should ever substitute one Lord for another, if the cross of Christ was replaced by any other cross, the gospel would be betrayed and the church judged. The next month, August of 1933, he sent a letter to his grandmother:

> It is becoming increasingly clear that what we are going to get is a big, popular national church whose nature cannot be reconciled with Christianity, and we must be prepared to enter upon entirely new paths which we shall have to tread. The conflict is really Germanism or Christianity and the sooner the conflict comes out in the open the better. Nothing could be more dangerous than its concealment.[3]

Bonhoeffer saw clearly what we in America have not yet grasped: that for us as Christians, the conflict is really between humanism and Christianity; or alternative religions and Christianity. On one side is a deteriorating culture and on the other side of the divide is the cross of Christ with its message of hope and redemption. For us as Christians it is really a struggle for the survival of the message of the cross in our increasingly hostile culture. If ever Christians need to be sharing the message of the gospel, "which is the power of God unto salvation," it is now.

THE POWER OF THE EARLY CHURCH

Think for a moment what the power of the gospel accomplished in the early centuries. With no political base in the Roman government, without any majority in the culture, the gospel changed the spiritual and moral climate of the Roman Empire. Christianity competed with paganism and, for the most part, won the hearts and minds of the populace. Christians were radicals in the best sense of the word—radically committed to community in worship, radically committed to serving their pagan neighbors, and radically committed to living out the implications of their redemption.

Without freedom of religion, without a media presence, and without the ability to redress the wrongs against them, the Christians discovered that the gospel had the power to change individuals, families, and the culture. Their faith was not in their beleaguered numbers but in a simple message that they unashamedly proclaimed. They were not intimidated by the odds against them but were invigorated by the power of the Spirit. For the most part, they stayed on message and the results proved it.

OUR OWN HIDDEN CROSS

Have we—I speak to those of us who are committed Christians—have we forgotten that God's power is more clearly seen in the message of the cross than in any political or social plan we might devise? Might not our search for some antidote to our grievous ills be symptomatic of our lost confidence in the power of the gospel to change people from the inside out? Do we cling to the cross with the deep conviction that it is not simply a part of our message to the world, but rightly understood it is the whole of it?

We have witnessed increasing hostility against Christianity from society in general and from state institutions in particular. The restraints of our Christian past are being cast aside with cynical arrogance. In an effort to be "relevant," we now face the temptation of being diverted from our mission and becoming involved doing what is good while bypassing what is best.

What, after all, is the meaning of the cross about which we speak? Why should Christians "cling to the old rugged cross," as the old hymn reminds us to do? Surely, we might think we have outgrown such sentimentality. But it is exactly here that Christianity stands or falls; it is the meaning of the cross that gives Christianity its power.

The cross is nothing less than the self-substitution of God for us. Because God chose to forgive sinful humans, He could only do so righteously. In the words of Charles E. Cranfield, He chose "to direct against his own very self in the person of his Son the full weight of that righteous wrath which they deserved."[4] God the Son paid the penalty for our sins to God the Father; thus "salvation is of the Lord."

THE CHRISTIAN CANNOT APPROACH THE CROSS WITH COOL DETACHMENT.

The Christian cannot approach the cross with cool detachment. The cross exposes the futility of all our self-righteousness; it reminds us that we are sinners incapable of bringing about our own reconciliation with God. Christ died to save sinners, to reveal the love of God, and to conquer evil. Before this cross we can only stand with bowed heads and broken spirits.

And herein comes the warning: P. T. Forsyth, when speaking of the cross as the focal point of God's work for sinners, wrote, "If you move faith from that centre, you have driven the nail into the Church's coffin. The Church is then doomed to death, and it is only a matter of time when she shall expire."[5] The church can only live and breathe at the cross; without it there is no life and no reason to exist.

Let me repeat Forsythe's warning: Without the cross we pound a nail into our coffin! There is a danger that we become so overburdened with social/political agendas that our message is lost amid our many cultural skirmishes. The church has always faced the temptation to modify the gospel or make it secondary to a given political, philosophical, or cultural agenda. When this happens, Christians have exposure to the culture, but the cross does not. Again, it is hidden.

Jacques Ellul, in *The Subversion of Christianity*, wrote, "Each generation thinks it has finally discovered the truth ... Christianity becomes an empty bottle that the successive cultures fill with all kinds of things."[6] Regrettably, today the Christian bottle has been filled with many different agendas: pop psychology, environmentalism, and a nationalist spirit that cannot distinguish between Christianity and the American way of life. The cross has become an ornament hung around the neck, not an instrument that changes the heart.

Some political activists have filled the Christian bottle with a strategy for political reform. Salvation, it appears, is electing conservatives to national and local office. Important though the right leaders might be, we must always remember that God is neither Republican nor Democrat. When the cross is wrapped in the flag of a political party, it is always distorted or diminished. Even for some who have experienced its power, the cross has become an addendum to what is thought to be more pressing agendas.

Here in America we have what many believe is a new phenomenon in the history of the church. In previous eras we have seen the gospel neglected or even mocked by religious liberals and nominal Christians—that is to be expected. What is different today is that the message of the cross is being ignored even by those who claim to be saved by its message. At the very time when the gospel must be proclaimed most clearly, we are hearing muffled voices even from some of the great evangelical pulpits of our land. Christian books flood our markets that have little to do with the heart of the Christian message.

Here are a few substitutes for the message of the gospel that I have observed:

- God wants you to experience physical healing.
- God wants you to be healthy and wealthy too.
- Jesus will help you be a better businessman, parent, entrepreneur, etc.
- God wants you to cheerily face life by knowing "God is for you"—whether you've repented of sin or not.
- God's will for you is good nutrition, physical exercise, and in general, living the good life.
- The message of Christianity is community—not the cross.

In the evangelical community, psychology is substituted for theology and cheap grace has replaced what Bonhoeffer described as "costly grace." In short, we have lost our intellectual and spiritual center and replaced it with consumerism, self-help, and the quest for personal advantage. We are self-absorbed rather than God-absorbed. And we can see the results.

A FINAL GLIMPSE OF GERMANY

The most discerning analysis that I've read about the failure of the church in Nazi Germany was given by an evangelical pastor who preached a moving sermon to his weary congregation. His words should cause us to stop and ponder their relevance to us in America.

In April 1945, amid the ruins of a defeated Germany, Helmut Thielicke, a German theologian and pastor, spoke movingly to his congregation in Stuttgart about the meaning of all that had happened. In a message that surely must have left his congregation spellbound, he, in effect, said that the nation got what it deserved because it had "repudiated forgiveness and kicked down the cross of the Lord."

In his powerful critique of what had gone wrong in a nation that was "Christian," Thielicke said that the cross of Christ had been neglected and thus the church was blinded to Germany's militarism. The church had overlooked its greatest danger, namely, that in gaining the whole world it might "lose its own soul." The heart of the matter, he said, was this: "Denying God and casting down the cross is never a merely private decision that concerns only my own inner life and my personal salvation, but this denial immediately brings the most brutal consequences for the whole of historical life and especially for our own people. 'God is not mocked.' The history of the world can tell us terrible tales based on that text."

In history, he says, the invisible is mightier than the visible. Anybody who still had not grasped that Germany with its program "was wrecked precisely on this dangerous rock called 'God' and nothing else has no eyes to see. Because he sees only individual catastrophes he no longer sees the basic, cardinal catastrophe behind them all."

Finally, he reminded his listeners that "the worship of success is generally the form of idol worship the devil cultivates most assiduously ... We could observe in the first years after

1933 the almost suggestive compulsion that emanates from great successes and how under the influence of these successes even Christians stopped asking in whose name and at what price they were achieved . . . Success is the greatest narcotic of all."[7]

Casting down the cross of Christ! Intoxicated with success! Substituting the temporary for the permanent! Thus was the church and the entire country crushed, crushed on the rock called God, "who is not mocked." Destroyed for being blinded by the pride of nationalism instead of being humbled by its great need for repentance. The church stood with pride, but it would not bow in humility. The church neglected the cross and had to live with the consequences.

IT'S OUR TURN

The Christian church has suffered throughout the centuries, and now it appears as if it is our turn. Like the early apostles, we will find that our commitment to share the gospel will run counter to the laws of the land. We must ask ourselves: At what point do we have to become lawbreakers rather than betray our faith? At what price are we willing to take the cross into the world and identify with our Savior? How do we both love the people of the world and yet oppose the agenda of those who would crush the gospel?

These are questions well beyond the scope of this chapter. But I believe it is time that we all began to live for eternity—not time, and for Christ—not ourselves. We must realize that our public effectiveness is largely based on our private relationship with God. The American church participates in many of the same sins as the world. Our passion for God is smothered, and our vision is marred. "Blessed are the pure in heart, for they shall see God," said Christ (Matthew 5:8).

When we come to the foot of the cross, it is there that we are finally broken; it is there that we learn to reach out to our confused and hurting world. The cross breaks down the barrier between us and the whole human race. Then we will no longer see ourselves as fighting the ACLU, the media, or the politicians. We must rid ourselves of the mentality that says, in effect, "If we just cleared all of them out, all would be well." Not so. As Os Guinness said, the problem with this view is "that there is no problem in the wider culture that you cannot see in spades in the Christian Church. The rot is in us, and not simply out there. And Christians are making a great mistake by turning everything into culture wars. It's a much deeper crisis."[8]

At last we come to the heart of the matter: the cross reminds us that the battle is not so much between church and state as it is within our own hearts. If Christ has all of us, if the cross stands above politics and the world as Bonhoeffer has reminded us, we shall overcome regardless of the cost.

As Christians we can welcome an assault on our freedoms as long as we see this conflict as an opportunity to bear an authentic witness for Christ. Without trivializing the great horror of what took place in Germany, it is nevertheless a fact that without suffering we would never have heard of a Niemoller or a Bonhoeffer or a Corrie ten Boom. Nor would we have read about thousands of courageous pastors, mothers, and fathers who kept living for God at great personal cost without any visible compensation in this life. Without suffering, God would not have seen their faith, which to Him is "more precious than gold."

We must be confident that Christ will set the record straight. Those who are faithful to Him and His cross will be rewarded with "joy unspeakable and full of glory." All rival crosses will be exposed and judged, and every knee shall bow and "every tongue confess that Jesus Christ is Lord, to the glory of God the Father."

Until then, God is glorified by our steadfastness. If we suffer faithfully, the cross will be exalted in the world. Bonhoeffer was right when he said *that it is before that cross and not before us that the world trembles.*

Sola Gloria!

NOTES

The Context of This Book

1. Viktor Frankl, *The Doctor and the Soul: Introduction to Logotherapy* (New York: Knopf, 1982), xxi; quoted in Ravi Zacharias, *Can Man Live Without God* (Dallas: Word, 1994), 25.

Chapter 1: When God Is Separated from Government, Judgment Follows

1. William L. Shirer, *The Rise and Fall of the Third Reich* (New York: Simon and Schuster, 1960), 234.

2. Deitmar Schmidt, *Pastor Niemoller* (New York: Doubleday, 1959), 94.

3. The eyewitness account was given to a pastor in an East Coast church who had just preached a message on abortion; he later shared it with me.

4. Schmidt, *Pastor Niemoller*, 72.

5. See Janet L. Folger, *The Criminalization of Christianity* (Sisters, Ore.: Multnomah, 2005). This book gives the details of how all public expressions of the Christian faith in the public sphere are deemed as crimes by groups such as the ACLU.

6. For a detailed discussion of the rights of public schools see John W. Whitehead, *The Rights of Religious Persons in Public Education*, 2d ed. (Wheaton, Ill.: Crossway, 1994).

7. Ibid.

8. John W. Whitehead, *Religious Apartheid: The Separation of Religion from American Public Life* (Chicago: Moody, 1994), 33.

9. As quoted in Whitehead, *Religious Apartheid*, on an opening unnumbered page.

10. Whitehead, *Religious Apartheid*, 22.

11. Ibid., 35.

12. Ibid., 36.

13. Ibid.

14. C. S. Lewis, "The Humanitarian Theory of Punishment," *God in the Dock* (Grand Rapids: Eerdmans, 1971), 292–93.

15. "Florida Principal, Athletic Director Could Go to Jail for Prayer Before Lunch at School," 15 August 2009, accessed at http://www.foxnews.com /story/0,2933,539741,00.html.

16. Richard Land, *The Divided States of America?* (Nashville: Thomas Nelson, 2007), 185.

17. Quoted in J. S. Conway, *The Nazi Persecution of the Churches 1933–1945* (New York: Basic, 1968), on an opening unnumbered page.

Chapter 2: It's Always the Economy

1. Gerald Suster, *Hitler: The Occult Messiah* (New York: St. Martin's, 1981), 135.

2. William Shirer, *The Rise and Fall of the Third Reich* (New York: Simon and Schuster, 1960), 239–40.

3. Quoted in Glenn Beck, *Common Sense* (New York: Mercury Radio Arts/Threshold Editions, 2009), 23–24. See also www.jeffersonblog. history.org/should-government-regulate-banks.

4. Richard Land, *The Divided States of America?* (Nashville: Nelson, 2007), 183.

5. Abraham Lincoln, 1864 address at a Sanitary Fair, Baltimore, Maryland, 18 April.

6. David A. Raush, *A Legacy of Hatred* (Chicago: Moody, 1984), 72.

7. John Whitehead, *Religious Apartheid* (Chicago: Moody, 1994), 38–39.

Chapter 3: That Which Is Legal Might Also Be Evil

1. Quoted in Joachim C. Fest, *Hitler* (New York: Harcourt, 1973), 212.

2. Quoted in Shirer, *The Rise and Fall of the Third Reich* (New York: Simon and Schuster, 1960), 268.

3. R. J. Rushdoony, *Law and Liberty* (Fairfax, Va.: Thoburn, 1971), 33.

4. Shirer, *The Rise and Fall*, 238.

5. J. Noakes and G. Pridham, eds., *Nazism: A History in Documents and Eyewitness Accounts, 1919–1945*, vol. 1 (New York: Schocken Books, 1983), 476.

6. Quoted in John Warwick Montgomery, *The Law Above the Law* (Minneapolis: Bethany, 1975), 25–26.

7. Speech to the Consititutional Convention, June 28, 1787, www.saferschools.org/pdfs/Franklin.pdf. Franklin was age eighty-one at the time; see also www.loc.gov/exhibits/religion/rel06.html.

8. Cited in John W. Whitehead, *The Second American Revolution*, (Elgin Ill.: Cook, 1982), 46–47.

9. C. Gregg Singer, *A Theological Interpretation of American History*, quoted in Whitehead, *The Second American Revolution*, 34.

10. Whitehead, *The Second American Revolution*, 46–47.

11. Quoted in Whitehead, *The Second American Revolution*.

12. Ibid., 51.

13. Ibid.

14. Montgomery, *The Law Above the Law*, 54–55.

15. Quoted in John Whitehead, *The Stealing of America* (Westchester Ill.: Crossway, 1983), 32.

16. Quoted in Janet Folger, *The Criminalization of Christianity* (Sisters, Ore.: Multnomah, 2005), 99.

Chapter 4: Propaganda Can Change a Nation

1. Adolf Hitler, *Mein Kampf*, Ralph Manheim, trans. (Boston: Houghton Mifflin, 1943), 583.

2. Ibid.

3. Ibid., 479.

4. Ibid.

5. Richard Terrell, *Resurrecting the Third Reich* (Shreveport, La.: Huntington House, 1994), 176.

6. Janet L. Folger, *The Criminalization of Christianity* (Sisters, Ore.: Multnomah, 2005), 75.

7. Hitler, *Mein Kamph*, 231.

8. Ibid., 276.

9. Marshall Kirk and Hunter Madsen, *After the Ball* (New York: Plume, 1990), as quoted in Alan Sears and Craig Osten, *The Homosexual Agenda* (Nashville: B & H), 18–19.

10. Ibid., 20.

11. Sears and Osten, *The Homosexual Agenda*, 22.

12. Kirk and Madsen, *After the Ball*, as quoted in Sears and Osten, *The Homosexual Agenda*, 22.

13. Ibid., 23.

14. Ibid., 26–27.

15. Ibid., 27.

16. Sears and Osten, *The Homosexual Agenda*, 48.

17. As quoted in *Time*, 23 December 1940, 38.

18. See "MP Geert Wilders, Chairman, Netherlands Party for Freedom, 25 September 2008, at www.facingjihad.commp-geert-wilders-chairman-netherlands-party-for-freedom.

19. Janet L. Folger, *The Criminalization of Christianity*, 28–29.

20. See Jim Boulet Jr. "Obama Declares War on Conservative Talk Radio," www.americanthinker.com/2008/11obama-declares-war-on-conserva.html.

Chapter 5: Parents—Not the State—Are Responsible for a Child's Training

1. Michael P. Donnelly, "Germany—It's Time for Some Change" in HSLDA—The Home School Court Report, vol. 25, no.1, Jan./Feb. 2009, 8.

2. Dana Hanley, "Courage and Conviction—The Struggle for Home Schooling Freedom in Germany," www.homeschoolenrichment.com, March/April, 2007, 36.

3. Ibid., 39.

4. Quoted in Duane Lester, "The Threats to Homeschooling: From Hitler to the NEA," 11 August 2008, at http://www.allamericanblogger.com/3415/the-threats-to-homeschooling-from-hitler-to-the-nea/.

5. Ibid.

6. Ibid.

7. Jeremy Noakes and Geoffery Pridham, eds., *Nazism: A History in Documents and Eyewitness Accounts, 1919–1945*, vol. 1 (New York: Schocken, 1983), 432.

8. Ibid., 437.

9. Ibid., 446.

10. Ibid., 427.

11. Ibid., 441.

12. Ibid., 429.

13. Ibid., 439.

14. Ibid., 422.

15. Ibid., 423.

16. Ibid., 428.

17. Ibid.

18. Ibid., 446.

19. Quoted in William M. Bowen, *Globalism: America's Demise* (Lafayette, La.: Huntington House, 1984), 19–20.

20. Marlin Maddoux, *Public Education Against America* (New Kensington, Penna.: Whitaker House, 2006), 84.

21. Ibid., 80–88.

22. Ibid., 134.

23. "Fox News Reporting: Do You Know What Textbooks Your Children Are Reading?" 4 September 2009, www.foxnews.com/story/0,2993,545900,00 .html

24. Tammy Bruce, *The Death of Right and Wrong* (Roseville, Calif.: Prima Publishing, 2003), 88.

25. Ibid., 195.

26. Maddox, *Public Education*, 141–42.

27. http://www.foxnews.com/story/0,2933,545900,00.html.

28. Dinesh D'Souza, *Illiberal Education* (New York: Free Press, 1991), 9–10.

29. Tim Stafford, "Campus Christians and the New Thought Police" *Christianity Today*, 10 February 1992, 17.

30. Maddox, *Public Education*, 29.

31. Ibid., 65.

32. Quoted in Maddox, *Public Education*, 65.

33. Maddox, *Public Education*, 69.

Chapter 6: Ordinary Heroes Can Make a Difference

1. Dietrich Bonhoeffer, *The Cost of Discipleship*, trans. C. Kaiser (New York: Macmillan, 1949), 43, 45.

2. Tim Stafford, "Campus Christians and the New Thought Police," *Christianity Today*, 10 February 1992, 19.

3. Cited in Eberhard Bethge, *Bonhoeffer: Exile and Martyr* (New York: Seabury, 1975), 155.

4. Corrie ten Boom and Elizabeth and John Sherrill (1971; repr., Grand Rapids: Baker, 2006), 115.

5. This is a summary of a longer article on the subject in *Kindred Spirit*, Winter/Spring 2009, vol. 33, no.1. p.12, "Taking the Long View."

6. Sheldon Vanauken, *A Severe Mercy* (New York: Harper Collins, 1977), 85.

7. Bonhoeffer, *The Cost of Discipleship*, 258.

Chapter 7: We Must Exalt the Cross in the Gathering Darkness

1. Eberhard Bethge, *Dietrich Bonhoeffer* (New York: Harper &Row, 1970), 228.

2. Mary Bosanquet, *The Life and Death of Dietrich Bonhoeffer* (London: Hodder & Stoughton, 1968), 121–22.

3. Bethge, *Dietrich Bonhoeffer*, 232.

4. Quoted in John Stott, *The Cross of Christ* (Downers Grove, Ill.: InterVarsity, 1986), 134.

5. Quoted in Stott, *The Cross of Christ*, 48.

6. Jacques Ellul, *The Subversion of Christianity* (Grand Rapids: Eerdmans, 1986), 18.

7. Helmut Thielicke, "The Great Temptation," *Christianity Today*, 12 July, 1985, 24–31. My summary in this chapter is adapted from this longer version.

8. As quoted in "Religion and Politics: A Round Table Discussion," *Modern Reformation*, September/October 1994, 25.

MORE BOOKS BY
ERWIN W. LUTZER

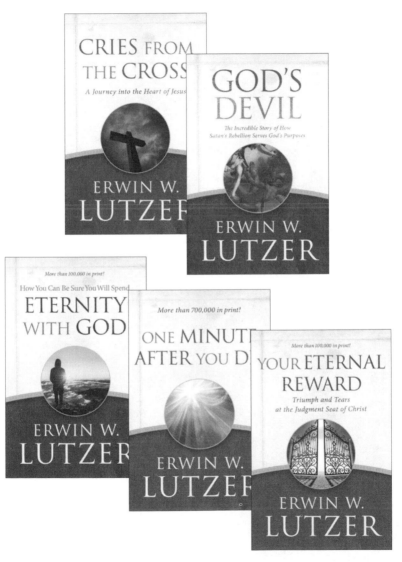

MOODY
Publishers™

From the Word to Life

THE STORY OF NAZI GERMANY IS ONE OF CONFLICT BETWEEN TWO SAVIORS AND TWO CROSSES.

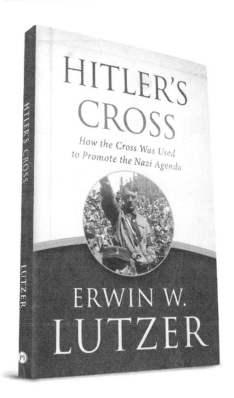

H*itler's Cross* is the story of a nation whose church forgot its call and discovered its failure way too late. Outlining critical lessons from Hitler's hold on the German church, it is a cautionary tale for every church and Christian to remember who the true King is.

MOODY
Publishers™

From the Word to Life

MOODYMEDIA.ORG
DECADES OF TEACHING
AT YOUR FINGERTIPS

- Ask
- Listen
- Download
- Share
- Read
- Shop

From the Word **to Life**

Moody Radio produces and delivers compelling programs filled with biblical insights and creative expressions of faith that help you take the next step in your relationship with Christ.

You can hear Moody Radio on 36 stations and more than 1,500 radio outlets across the U.S. and Canada. Or listen on your smartphone with the Moody Radio app!

www.moodyradio.org